"HETEROGENIUS" CLASSROOMS

Detracking Math & Science

A Look at Groupwork in Action

Produced by
Maika Watanabe

—DVD CONTENTS—

This DVD contains Subtitles for the Deaf and Hard of Hearing

"HETEROGENIUS" CLASSROOMS

Detracking Math and Science

A Look at Groupwork in Action

"HETEROGENIUS" CLASSROOMS

Detracking Math and Science

A Look at Groupwork in Action

Edited by

Maika Watanabe

Teachers College
Columbia University
New York and London

Production of film and book made possible in part by grants from: The Spencer Foundation; Professional Development Council, San Francisco State University; Center for Science and Mathematics Education, San Francisco State University; Office of the Dean, College of Education, San Francisco State University

Published by Teachers College Press, 1234 Amsterdam Avenue, New York, NY 10027

ISBN 978-0-8077-5246-3

Printed on acid-free paper

Manufactured in the United States of America

19 18 17 16 15 14 13 12 8 7 6 5 4 3 2 1

For Ayumi, Kaito, and Brad

Contents

FOREWORD
A thank you note to the educators—adults and youth— of *"Heterogenius" Classrooms*

Michelle Fine

Just when I was despairing about oil spills, war, global capitalism, neo-liberalism, Racing to the Top, I popped *"Heterogenius" Classrooms* into my computer and felt a warm calm. This video will not fix the oil spill, stop the wars, or restore the economy, but it does return the educational conversation back to fundamental questions posed by DuBois, Dewey, and Greene, by Oakes, Moses and Ladson-Billings about educational debt, justice, and the transformative power of detracking.

Peering into science and math classrooms to bear witness to the transformative possibilities of detracking, *"Heterogenius" Classrooms* offers wide-angle inspiration and explicit zoom-in on details of practice. The blend of classroom scenes and interviews with students, educators, and university researchers unfolds a doubled message. Through accessible language and detailed illustrations, these very fine educators carefully reveal the "magic" but also the "how-to's" of rigorous curricula, complex tasks, and deep classroom participation. At the same time, as political actors on the 21st-century education stage, *"Heterogenius"* educators boldly insist on detracked education as a human right for all children.

In these days of edu-speak about standards, racing to the top (and most falling off), gifted and talented programs, selective admissions, privately managed schools . . . and other gentrified public schools, these educators weave together a story about beakers, lab experiments, equations, physics, anxiety, boys with hidden academic desire and girls who "hate science!" with a story about racial and ethnic justice, democracy, and access as key elements of everyday schooling. We come to see—in flesh, conversation, collaboration, and relationships—how science and math serve as gateways—check points—to lives of meaning and purpose. We learn how to design complex tasks and groupwork in ways that engage together those students who have always enjoyed academic success and those for whom failure has been their academic home.

Watching this video, you will remember the electricity and sensuality of education as it should be—messy, democratic, collective, inquiry based, noisy, frustrating, giggly, and engaged; a respite for the obsessive "ringing in the ears" of ranking, sorting, measuring, and segregating.

Maika Watanabe, the film's producer, takes seriously the very notions of accountability, rigor, and achievement that float around educational discussions, often hollow and usually punitive. Through the bodies and words of youth and adults, she has produced a film about the democratic values of teaching and learning and the capacity of adults and youth to reimagine tomorrow. Three values anchor the film, bringing to life the vision, the labor, and the educational contexts for detracking.

Radical Desire to Expand the Pool of Smarts: One educator tells us that the task of detracking is expanding the pool of the best and brightest, so that "success is a bountiful harvest that more children can enjoy." At its heart, this video is an invitation to challenge the sorting, segregating, and the privileging of some "smarts" over others. These educators design, instead, classrooms that boil over with wisdom, creativity, original solutions—the very base of creative science. *This is the vision of detracking.*

Intentionality: "We can't be complacent about status hierarchies," explains Watanabe. We must intend to disrupt them. For the boy who enters with a hood on his head, and his head on the desk, we must "assign competence; catch him at a moment of intellectual clarity and originality" and name his contribution. These educators and youth view detracking as a project of educational justice and practice that requires a deliberate commitment to interrupt the passive reproduction of inequality and status hierarchies. *This is the labor of detracking.*

Collaboration with Colleagues/Among Students: Detracking is not a solo flight—for students or educators. Swimming against the stream of individualism, miseducation, academic despair, and privilege—you'll need buddies. Groupwork, complex problems, public assignation of competence, feedback from colleagues, a culture that supports multiple abilities are all critical ingredients for the detracking recipe. Find good colleagues and a creative principal, and then build a culture of inquiry, collaboration, support, and experimentation. *This is the educational culture in which detracking flourishes and can be sustained.*

Why Now?

It's simply refreshing to watch *"Heterogenius"* in these days of testing mania, scientifically validated segregation, growing gifted and talented programs, proliferations of selective admissions high schools, creamy charters and contract schools, an ever widening education gap contoured along the fault lines of race and class. "*Heterogenius*" speaks the long buried desire to educate all young people with complexity, inquiry, and challenge.

Many of us have written theoretically about the virtues of detracking and empirically about the democratic impact for high-achieving and low-achieving students. No one has taken this on in science and math to reveal, in film, the sweet and brilliant and delicate art of teaching in a detracked class. Until now. Thanks, Maika and all of your educator and student colleagues, for a film that provokes an imagination for educational justice on the ground, in the classroom, with educators and youth, across the rich space of diversity and heterogenius.

CHAPTER 1

Introduction

Maika Watanabe

Academic researchers have documented the problems of tracking and the promise of detracking reform through theory and research; however, many pre-service and in-service teachers remain perplexed by how to teach students with a wide range of academic skills, so that all students are challenged with the same college-bound curricula, especially in math and science. The film, *"Heterogenius" Classrooms,* addresses this gap between theory and practice by visually showcasing teachers and students sharing and experiencing best practices in detracked math and science classrooms.

This book features the backdrop to the film. Chapters 2–5 provide lesson plans, student handouts, rubrics, and reflections written by featured teachers in order of their appearance in the film. Chapter 6 details the many supports for struggling students as well as the professional development opportunities for teachers that make it possible for teachers to enact the innovative and challenging curricula. Chapter 7 addresses frequently asked questions that I encounter when showing this film to pre-service and in-service teachers, administrators, teacher educators, and professors. Chapter 8 concludes with additional resources on detracking reform.

While I wrote the book to complement the film, this book will also be of general interest to professors, administrators, and teachers interested in effective curricula and pedagogy for heterogeneous classrooms. Professors who teach Curriculum and Instruction courses might assign the lesson plan chapters to inspire their students to "think outside the box" of traditional, teacher-centered lesson plans. Education professors in educational leadership and school reform would be interested in examining school-level and district-level supports necessary to sustain detracked schools with their graduate students. District and school-level administrators could use information on teacher professional development in Chapter 6 to inform their thinking about how to support teachers embarking on detracking reform. They might also use the lesson plan chapters as starting points for discussion among teachers in professional development meetings. School-site administrators would also gain from reading more about the focused curricular offerings and support classes described in Chapter

6. Finally, teacher leaders, who are tired of witnessing poor instruction in tracked classrooms, might use this book in a book group of like-minded colleagues to begin a detracking movement from the ground up.

Why Should I Care About Detracking? What's Wrong with Tracking?

There are three main problems with tracking. First, research consistently demonstrates that students in lower-tracked classes are not afforded the same quality of instruction as students in higher-tracked classes. They get the least-experienced teachers, they do work that does not exercise critical thinking skills, and they experience low expectations, even from well-meaning teachers (Finley, 1984; Oakes, 2005; Page, 1991). The gaps in skills and content knowledge across tracks grow over time, making movement from low- to high-tracked classes virtually impossible without additional support.

Secondly, the assignment practices are very problematic. Many researchers argue that tracking plays a central role in perpetuating race- and class-based inequality in American society as students of color and/or students from low socioeconomic backgrounds are disproportionately assigned to the lower academic tracks, irrespective of academic achievement (Mickelson, 1999; Lucas, 1999). There are also studies that document how privileged parents use their power to place their children in higher tracks even when these students did not qualify, undermining the pedagogical rationale for tracking (Wells & Serna, 1996).

Third, many researchers question traditional notions of ability and intelligence that underlie the tracking assignments. How can educators assign students to tracks when ability is not fixed, innate, unidimensional, or easily assessed (Oakes, Wells, Jones, & Datnow, 1997)? When should the assignment practice start, and should "late bloomers" be relegated to inadequate educational opportunities in the low track? Research reporting that it is extremely rare for students to move up tracks once they are assigned to the lower tracks compounds the impact of placement decisions (Lucas, 1999).

Defenders say that problems with tracking lie in ineffective implementation. They say that educators need to improve the quality of instruction across tracks and implement fair assignment practices (Hallinan, 1994). Students in my teacher education courses often ask me if I would support tracking if the quality of low-tracked classes was better, and if the assignment practices were fair. My answer: No. It would be better, but it would still result in inequitable instructional opportunities. The hierarchical nature of grouping practices always privileges one group of students over another, and students internalize and meet teacher and peer expectations for student performance. In addition, efforts to improve tracking practices have been tried and more often than not failed in typical public schools.

Why Is Detracking Math and Science Important?

Algebra and Chemistry/Physics Are Gate Keepers to College. Taking algebra in eighth or ninth grades and chemistry or physics before graduating from high school is essential for students to complete the advanced math and science sequence of courses that fulfill college prerequisite requirements. While students in the high track take these courses and continue with an advanced course of study in math and science, less proficient students in the low track often start a math sequence that begins with pre-algebra or other remedial math course and end their high school careers with at best two years of college preparatory math (Burris, Heubert, & Levin, 2004). In addition, these students often do not take more than one year of laboratory science (Blank & Langesen, 2005). This lower-level sequence precludes these students' opportunities to enroll in four-year institutions of higher education, which require at least three years of college preparatory mathematics (Algebra 1, Geometry, Algebra 2) and two years of laboratory science (biology, chemistry, or physics). An especially troubling aspect of this bifurcated curriculum is that Black and Latino students and students from low socioeconomic backgrounds are disproportionately underrepresented in the college-bound sequence of courses (Blank & Langesen, 2005).

Detracking Increases Enrollment in College-bound Math and Science Classes. Researchers report that detracking has led to a dramatic increase in the percentage of students successfully completing the college-preparatory math and science sequence of classes at the high school level with gains for all groups of students—including initial low and high achievers as well as

Table 1.1. Groupworthy Task Features in Teachers' Lessons

Groupworthy Task Features	Physics of Music	Perimeter Challenges	The New Swimming Pool	Inter-molecular Forces
Big Idea	X	X	X	X
Multiple Ability	X	X	X	X
Open-Ended	X	X	X	X
Interdependence	X	X	X	X
Individual Accountability		X	X	X
Assessment	X	X	X	X

Figure 1.1. Features of a Groupworthy Task

Big Idea: Is the organizing concept or big idea—a big idea indeed? How do you know? How central is the concept to the discipline?

Multiple Abilities: Do the resources incorporate multiple representations/ways of understanding/ways of presenting information? Is there a tight connection between the resources and the activity? What are the multiple intellectual abilities called upon to access and/or to complete the task?

Open-endedness: What is the problem to be solved in the activity? Is there a right or wrong answer, or an "expected" answer? (Is the answer "It depends?") Are there different ways of arriving at a possible solution?

Interdependence: Is there enough to do for a group? Is the activity rich and complex? Is there a group product? What is the relationship between the group product and the discussion questions? What is the relationship between the group product and the resources? Are there group data collected among members? How is the group discussion essential for producing a quality product?

Individual Accountability: Are individual reports included in the activity? Are they tightly connected to the activity and/or to the big idea/central concept? How will the group discussion become critical for a student completing the individual report?

Assessment: Are there clear evaluation criteria for group product and group process? How are they stated? How will you assess what students are learning as they complete this activity?

Source: Lotan, R. (2007). [Features of a Groupworthy Task.] Unpublished Handout.

students of diverse racial and socioeconomic backgrounds. Burris, Heubert, and Levin (2006) offer compelling research evidence that detracking helps all students. In a 6-year longitudinal study of students in the Rockville Centre School District in New York, these researchers compared the math achievement of three sixth-grade cohorts who learned math in a tracked setting with three sixth-grade cohorts who learned in a detracked setting. They report a statistically significant increase in the percentages of students who took math courses beyond Algebra 2 in high school for every subgroup: students from low socioeconomic backgrounds (32% to 67%), Black and Latino students (46% to 67%), initial low achievers (38% to 53%), average achievers (81% to 91%), and high achievers (89% to 99%). The mean standardized test scores of high-achieving students who learned in the detracked setting were statistically indistinguishable from comparable students learning in the tracked environment. In addition, more high-achieving students who learned in the detracked environment took the AP Calculus exam and scored higher than their counterparts in the tracked environment. These results led these researchers to conclude that not only are high-achieving students performing better in mathematics, but that more students have become high achievers.

Dr. Carol Burris, scholar and visionary principal of South Side High School, and her dedicated team of teachers and administrators gradually expanded the school district's detracking efforts across different subjects at the high school level. The year-of-entry 2001 cohort was the first cohort to be heterogeneously grouped in all subjects, including math and science, in the ninth grade. During the 2005–2006 school year, heterogeneous grouping was extended into the tenth grade. Burris, Welner, Wiley, and Murphy (2008) compared three tracked cohorts with three detracked cohorts in their attainment of two diplomas (International Baccalaureate and New York Regents) that require rigorous course-taking and assessments far beyond those required for the local high school diploma. Most 4-year universities recognize International Baccalaureate (IB) courses as equivalent to or exceeding Advanced Placement (AP) coursework. Racial and socioeconomic demographic data remained stable across this time period. The researchers found that

> being a member of a detracked cohort was associated with an increase of roughly 70% in the odds of IB diploma attainment and a much greater increase in the odds of Regents diploma attainment—ranging from a three-fold increase for White or Asian students, to a five-fold increase for African American or Latino students who were eligible to receive free or reduced price lunch, to a 26-fold increase for African American or Latino students not eligible for free or reduced-price lunch. Further, even as the enrollment in IB classes increased, average scores remained high. (Burris et al., 2008, p. 572)

Detracking led to an increase in the numbers of students overall who successfully completed advanced-level high school classes, and who thereby fulfilled or exceeded 4-year university admission requirements. Subsequent research into the Class of 2009, which was the first detracked cohort in all subject areas through the end of the tenth grade, showed that 85% of the students elected to take IB English and IB math (Garrity & Burris, 2007). The approach of school-level leaders in the district was more rigor with support, not remediation through tracking.

Teacher to Teacher: Creating Groupworthy Tasks

The next four chapters feature teachers' lesson plans, which I hope will be of use to teachers writing their own lesson plans for heterogeneous classrooms. Teachers reflected on the challenges they faced enacting the lesson and how they would improve upon the lesson plan.

As mentioned in the film, not all teachers used complex instruction in their teaching; Maja Catipovic, in particular, did not create the Physics of Music unit with the complex instruction framework in mind. Nonetheless, her unit shared similar tenets with features of a groupworthy task, as Table 1.1 illustrates. In the case of the individual accountability feature, Catipovic reflects that including an individual assessment would have improved her unit plan.

Dr. Rachel Lotan created a quick review sheet for her students in the Stanford Teacher Education Program as they set out to write their first groupworthy tasks (see Figure 1.1). With her permission, I include it in this chapter as a helpful guide for readers to consult as they develop their own groupworthy tasks.

A frequent misconception about detracking is that teachers must "teach to the middle." Lesson plans featured in Chapters 2–5 counter this notion. Although it seems counterintuitive, these math and science teachers have raised the bar higher to create units that are deeply challenging for all students, including those who were formerly high tracked. The tasks require a different set of "smarts" that no student has individually, so students have to work with others to solve the problem. There is a fear that previously high-tracked students will lose out in detracked classrooms, but what I hear over and over from students in these teachers' classes is that they are all challenged. They realize that everyone has strengths and weaknesses, and they draw on the collective "smarts" of the people in their group to solve problems.

Vision, Tenacity, and True Belief in Students

I have been incredibly inspired by the detracked schools I have visited in the last 10 years. In addition to the film's featured schools and South Side High School in Rockville Centre, New York, the Preuss School is a detracked school for first-generation college students in San Diego, CA, 94% of whose students in the Class of 2009 were admitted to 4-year universities. Staff members at these detracked schools do not just give lip service to high expectations. There is a consistent message at the schools from faculty, administrators, and students that students can all achieve at the highest levels. Their vision, tenacity, and belief in students shine. In stark contrast, tracking puts ceilings on student opportunities to grow.

We need to actively turn the tide against the ill effects of tracking. Otherwise, we are just part of the problem. The need is urgent and we cannot wait for the stars to align before taking action. How many more generations of students will we subject to something that has not worked, when there is a promising reform out there? Small steps can build detracking efforts. Take them.

References

Blank, R. K., & Langesen, D. (2005). *State indicators of science and mathematics education 2005.* Washington, DC: Council of Chief State School Officers.

Burris, C. C., Heubert, J. P., & Levin, H. M. (2004). Math acceleration for all. *Educational Leadership, 61*(5): 68–71.

Burris, C. C., Heubert, J. P., & Levin, H. M. (2006). Accelerating mathematics achievement using heterogeneous grouping. *American Educational Research Journal, (Spring):* 105–136.

Burris, C. C., Welner, K., Wiley, E., & Murphy, J. (2008). Accountability, rigor and detracking: Challenging curricula as a universal good for all students. *Teachers College Record, 110*(3), 571–607.

Finley, M. K. (1984). Teachers and tracking in a comprehensive high school. *Sociology of Education (57),* 233–243.

Garrity, D. L., & Burris, C. C. (2007). Personalized learning in detracked classrooms. *School Administrator, 8*(64). Retrieved November 4, 2010, from http://www.aasa.org/SchoolAdministratorArticle.aspx?id=6532

Hallinan, M. T. (1994). Tracking: From theory to practice. *Sociology of Education, 67* (2), 79–91.

Lucas, S. R. (1999). *Tracking inequality.* New York: Teachers College Press.

Mickelson, R. A. (1999). *The effects of tracking, within-school segregation, and racially identifiable African American schools on student outcomes in the Charlotte-Mecklenburg School District: A report to the U. S. District Court for the Western District of North Carolina in the case of Capacchione v. Charlotte-Mecklenburg Schools et al., Charlotte, North Carolina.*

Oakes, J. (2005). *Keeping track.* New Haven, CT: Yale University Press.

Oakes, J., Wells, A. S., Jones, M., & Datnow, A. (1997). Detracking: The social construction of ability, cultural politics, and resistance to reform. *Teachers College Record, 98*(3), 482–510.

Page, R. (1991). *Lower-track classrooms: A curricular and cultural perspective.* New York: Teachers College Press.

Wells, A. S., & Serna, I. (1996). The politics of culture: Understanding local political resistance to detracking in racially mixed schools. *Harvard Educational Review, 66* (1), 93–119.

CHAPTER 2

Physics of Music Unit

Maja Catipovic

The Physics of Music Unit is one half of the Waves and Light group of physics standards, which took us a total of 6 to 8 weeks. Prior to the music unit, we had studied electromagnetic waves, primarily light and optics, mostly through experiments. The physics of music unit took us 4 weeks of in-class time, but it can easily be done in a different configuration if you do not have the time in class; for example, you can teach the introductory activities in class for two weeks, then have students work on instruments exclusively at home/after school (see Curriculum—Lesson Sequence for more details on the introductory activities).

The Musical Instrument Project is the culminating activity for the wave topic. Students construct a musical instrument, either on their own or with partners. As they work, they assemble a portfolio documenting their process, showing the calculations involved, and justifying the notes their instruments ultimately play. The last day consisted of presentations: Students talked through their trials and tribulations and had to play a tune demonstrating a full octave range on the instrument. I gave students two weeks of in-class time (block periods) every day to work on their instruments. Some groups finished early and others needed extended after-school time.

School Context

This unit was adapted from a project developed by David R. Lapp at Mt. Tamalpais High School in Marin County (visit his website: http://staff.tamhigh.org/lapp/#/home). He used this project for about 15 years with seniors in his AP Physics class, and then conducted workshops for teachers where he shared his exquisitely detailed materials and experience.

My institutional context was quite different from that of David Lapp. I taught at High Tech High Bayshore, the Redwood City branch of the successful group of charter schools focused on science, technology, group-work, and projects. My students were ninth graders, enrolled in a 2-hour block of Math 1/Physics, both taught by me. The idea was that students would learn math in context through applications in science. My students were quite heterogeneous in math and science skill sets, interest in the subject (Physics was required), and interest in school, whereas his twelfth-grade students were uniformly interested in physics, since his students elected to take AP Physics.

This was my second year teaching physics (and my third year as a teacher). The year before I taught waves only in a cursory way, using worksheets. I was still figuring out what was appropriate for my students, given their grade level and backgrounds.

The biggest gift of my context was the amount of freedom given to teachers to shape the curricula. I chose to focus on the standards that I believed would be more accessible to ninth graders, and spent less time on electricity and magnetism, which my students found very abstract and difficult. I spent a lot of time bridging the abstract parts of physics with phenomena we could observe and get our hands on. This project was a very good example of my approach.

Materials and Costs

The materials needed for the activities and project were very specific, but not as expensive as I thought, with one exception. For the introductory activities I needed a lot of materials, so that each student could experience building each type of instrument before making a choice for his/her own project. I chose to provide each pair of students with the materials, although I think it would also be effective to have students work in groups of four, which would require half the materials.

Materials. PVC pipe, copper pipe (the exception—very expensive!—maybe another metal would work instead), wood; student workbooks containing the introductory activities outlined under the Curriculum—Lesson Sequence heading.

Equipment. PVC and pipe cutters, power tools for cutting and shaping wood, and one large, expensive hole puncher for puncturing holes in the copper for wind instruments; decibel meter, frequency meter (to determine the note being played—can be downloaded onto a computer), and a collection of sound files illustrating different frequencies and timbres of instruments.

Suggestions. If you have a shop class at your institution, you may be able to collaborate and share some of this equipment. Since we were a new charter school, we did not have a shop class.

Money. I asked for help from parents of students enrolled in my class—maybe you could ask your PTA for specific larger ticket items. One parent donated almost all of the wood from scraps he could not use

> in his carpentry shop. Nearby industrial businesses were happy to donate materials as well. For example, I got a whole class supply of mirrors, cut to my specifications, as well as metal cutters. I believe the businesses could receive tax deductions for the donations.

The rest of the supplies were covered by a grant of about $1,500 from the Peninsula Community Foundation. The application process was very straightforward and only took a couple days for me to complete (I basically wrote up a lesson plan). I highly encourage others to try writing grants at least once—there is money out there, especially now that school budgets are shrinking. Also, the money covered the basic workshop setup, which would be re-used every year. Only about a third of the supplies would need to be replenished every year, to provide new building supplies to each group of students.

Student Engagement in a Heterogeneous Math/Science Context

The motivation and skill sets of my students varied greatly. I had some motivated students with high skill sets, and some less motivated and frustrated students, with all permutations in between. Many had gaps in their math background that needed to be bridged in order for them to succeed.

I had students who were not skilled in paper-and-pencil settings but excelled here because of the nature of the hands-on work. For example, some of my students demonstrated high skills in building or working with tools and teaching others, whereas they did not have high math skills. This project increased their status in the class and allowed them to feel competent. One of the strengths of this lesson plan is that there are multiple entry points, and the nature of the groupwork allowed multiple intelligences to shine.

Because of this heterogeneity, I could not just conduct my class straight out of a textbook, as those differences between students would persist and create further frustration. Most projects and activities addressed basic understanding that was necessary for all, but were also open-ended, interesting at both the basic and extended, advanced levels.

The project was a great example of this framework. All students had basic requirements they had to meet that were fairly challenging. They needed to have an instrument that played an octave on key, and had to perform it in public on a fixed date! Students who were up to the challenge and could see themselves putting in extra time chose more difficult, elaborate instruments—some with more notes, others that were difficult to build or unique in configuration.

Nobody was bored! Students who finished early helped others who may have overextended themselves or worked on adding details to their work. Many were frustrated (there were breaking strings and snapping ukulele necks left and right), but they could use that information in their reports and presentations.

While there may be details to change for next time, I knew the project was a success when students presented their work to their classmates. The class demonstrated utmost respect and attention to their peers for a full 2 hours—a great achievement in any context but especially for these young, restless students. Cheers and applause permeated the air. After the unit's completion, all students had personal knowledge and understanding of the details of the frequencies of notes and scales, as well as the craftsmanship involved in constructing the instruments. All students seemed to have felt as though they had done something worthwhile, and if they had not been completely successful in the building of their instruments, they could articulate what to do differently and had advice and warnings for others.

Standards

The following content area standards were addressed in this unit:

California Physics Standards:

Waves

4. Waves have characteristic properties that do not depend on the type of wave. As a basis for understanding this concept:
   a. Students know waves carry energy from one place to another.
   c. Students know how to solve problems involving wavelength, frequency, and wave speed.
   d. Students know sound is a longitudinal wave whose speed depends on the properties of the medium in which it propagates.
   f. Students know how to identify the characteristic properties of waves: interference (beats), diffraction, refraction, Doppler effect, and polarization.

National Council for the Teaching of Mathematics (NCTM)

- judge the meaning, utility, and reasonableness of the results of symbol manipulations, including those carried out by technology
- analyze precision, accuracy and approximate error in measurement

National Science Teachers Association (NSTA)

More emphasis on:

- Process skills in context
- Using multiple process skills: manipulation, cognitive and procedural

- Public communication of work and student ideas to classmates
- Waves, including sound and seismic waves, have energy and can transfer energy when they interact with matter (we focused on the sound energy)

Given my students' age and ability, I think that if I were to do the project again I would spend more time after the instruments were due going back and solidifying their understanding of the concepts of how notes are put together into standard musical scales. The first time through, I think it was a very difficult concept that needed reinforcement. Reworking this information after the musical instrument project—after a concrete personal relationship with instruments—might have helped all students come to new understandings of these concepts.

Curriculum—Lesson Sequence

We worked on introductory activities in class for two weeks before embarking on the culminating activity, the instruments themselves. The idea was to introduce students to the theory of music in a hands-on way, to give them experience with notes, scales, and the building materials, and to build their confidence, so that they could make informed decisions about the types of instruments to build during their project. Students were introduced to the mathematical calculations that they needed to master during the first two weeks as well.

All of these activities were done in groups of two, given my small class size. In a larger class I would use groups of four, but I would suggest making sure that all students have a hand in calculating and doing the physical work as well.

Pages refer to David Lapp's book, *The Physics of Music and Musical Instruments,* which can be downloaded from his website (see Publications tab).

Day 1—Intro lecture: types of instruments, sound waves, formula sheet for calculating frequencies. I used many sound clips during the lecture.

Day 2—Graduated Cylinder Activity—our first instruments (graduated cylinders filled with different quantities of water produce different tones). This activity can be located on pp. 205–206 of his textbook, *Physics: An Introduction,* which can be downloaded from his website (see Textbook tab).

Day 3—Inquiry: Music Box Activity (pp. 107–109)—how do percussive instruments work? This was our first mechanical, physical experience with scales and notes.

Day 4—Guitar Investigation (pp. 67–69)—calculation activity; details of string instrument

Day 5 and 6—PVC Panpipes Construction (p. 96)—closed pipe wind instrument experience

Day 7, 8, 9—Copper Pipe Xylophone (p. 110)—percussion instrument experience

Day 10—Summary lecture, project intro, decision time for instrument type, planning

Assessment: Grading and Rubric

The project was graded in four parts: 1) an accumulation of points as students worked daily on their instruments and portfolio, 2) oral presentation, 3) quality of the instrument, and 4) engineer's portfolio (see Tables 2.1, 2.2, and 2.3). I include multipliers for scoring on two of the three rubrics. Not included on my first (and only—I no longer teach physics) try was a final test or quiz to assess their individual understanding. I would definitely add this next time, and use it as a way to plan backwards and check in on student understanding as they work. It would also serve as a guide for leading questions during lecture, class discussions, and portfolio assessment.

I would also refine the portfolio rubric and emphasize the importance of this artifact. Students started them well, but as the deadline for the presentation approached they were left behind, and I didn't emphasize it enough. This is a reflection of that fact that it was my first time through the project.

The last change I would add would be to find a way to assess students who worked in pairs separately—the best way may be to require individual portfolios. While this does increase the number of papers to grade, it would hold students accountable for their individual learning. In addition, there were several pairs of students who had difficulty collaborating fairly, where one partner did the majority of the building (often the male in a male/female pair), and I would like to discourage that, through an assessment technique like participation quizzes.

Author Note: Special thanks to Hillary Swanson, a teacher who taught at High Tech High Bayshore and High Tech High International, for sharing her rubrics with me. I modified two of her rubrics (Quality of Musical Instrument and Engineer's Portfolio) to include in this chapter.

Table 2.1. Oral Presentation Rubric

Category	4	3	2	1
Performance of Music		More advanced piece of music presented to class	Basic song played	No musical piece was played—only a scale or nothing
Physics of Sound: How does the instrument play notes?	Clearly placed in context, with explanation of sound waves and how to vary their pitch when constructing this instrument	Discussion not completely specific or clear, but accurate for your instrument	Very basic discussion of sound waves, not specific to your instrument	Acoustic properties of instrument not explained
Chronicle of the construction process: difficulties	Quick discussion of construction. Key assembly difficulttes identified and your solutions presented.		Solutions to difficulties not clear or specific	No discussion of difficulties, or how instrument was made
Advice			Clear summary of what to do differently next time	No insight provided
Collaboration Discussion			Summary of collaboration with your partner and how difficultties were resolved	No collaboration discussion

Table 2.2. Quality of Musical Instrument Rubric

Category	4	3	2	1
Stability X2	The instrument is sturdy and can be handled easily without breaking.	The instrument is sturdy and can be handled without breaking.	The instrument is sturdy enough to give a performance.	The instrument is somewhat sturdy.
Sound Quality X2	The instrument can be heard easily in a large room.	The instrument can be heard in a large room.	The instrument can be heard.	The instrument can be heard at times.
Engineering X4	The instrument plays a complete scale for which its structural components were calculated correctly.	The instrument plays a complete scale for which its structural components were calculated nearly correctly.	The instrument plays a complete scale. Its structural components may not match all calculations.	The instrument plays a complete scale.
Artistry X2	The instrument is very orderly and aesthetically pleasing.	The instrument is orderly and aesthetically pleasing.	The instrument is somewhat orderly or aesthetically pleasing.	The instrument is not orderly or aesthetically pleasing.

Table 2.3. Engineer's Portfolio Rubric

Category	4	3	2	1
Physics Explanation X4	The physics behind the instrument is thoroughly presented in a description that explains the words vibration, compression, rarefaction, longitudinal wave, amplitude, loudness, natural frequency, resonance, forced vibration, standing wave, crest, trough, and node.	The physics behind the instrument is presented in a description that explains the words vibration, compression, rarefaction, longitudinal wave, amplitude, loudness, natural frequency, resonance, forced vibration, standing wave, crest, trough, and node.	The physics behind the instrument is presented in a description that explains 9 of the following words: vibration, compression, rarefaction, longitudinal wave, amplitude, loudness, natural frequency, resonance, forced vibration, standing wave, crest, trough, and node.	The physics behind the instrument is presented in a description that explains 6 of the following words: vibration, compression, rarefaction, longitudinal wave, amplitude, loudness, natural frequency, resonance, forced vibration, standing wave, crest, trough, and node.
Diagrams X3	3 Diagrams are included: a Rough Draft Sketch, a 2nd Draft Illustration with dimensions, a Final Draft Illustration drawn to scale with dimensions. The final draft should include information of the dimensions of the note-producing elements. All are orderly and aesthetically pleasing.	3 Diagrams are included: a Rough Draft Sketch, a 2nd Draft Illustration with dimensions, a Final Draft Illustration drawn to scale with dimensions. The final draft should include information of the dimensions of the note-producing elements. All are somewhat orderly and aesthetically pleasing.	3 Diagrams are included: a Rough Draft Sketch, a 2nd Draft Illustration with dimensions, a Final Draft Illustration drawn to scale with dimensions. The final draft should include information of the dimensions of the note-producing elements.	3 Diagrams are included: a Rough Draft Sketch, a 2nd Draft Illustration with dimensions, a Final Draft Illustration drawn to scale with dimensions.

Calculations X2	The calculations for all 8 notes of the scale the instrument plays are included. The process is clearly laid out and the math is correct.	The calculations for all 8 notes of the scale the instrument plays are included. The math is correct.	The calculations for all 8 notes of the scale the instrument plays are included. The math is mostly correct.	The calculations for all 8 notes of the scale the instrument plays are included.
Procedure X3	The procedure is clearly presented to the public as either a paper, PPT, video, or pictorial set of diagrams. The medium of presentation is orderly and aesthetically pleasing. The procedure includes all of the following steps: research, design, construct, test, modify.	The procedure is presented to the public as either a paper, PPT, video, or pictorial set of diagrams. The medium of presentation is orderly and aesthetically pleasing. The procedure includes all of the following steps: research, design, construct, test, modify.	The procedure is presented to the public as either a paper, PPT, video, or pictorial set of diagrams. The procedure includes all of the following steps: research, design, construct, test, modify.	The procedure is presented to the public as either a paper, PPT, video, or pictorial set of diagrams. The procedure includes 3 of the following steps: research, design, construct, test, modify.

CHAPTER 3

Perimeter Challenge

Laura Evans

Perimeter Challenge is an adaptation of Activity 2.1B from *The Algebra Lab: Lab Gear Activities for Algebra 1* by Henri Picciotto, published by Creative Publications (see www.MathEdPage.org for more information). The San Lorenzo math department collaborates around curriculum and instruction to promote teacher growth and to better support heterogeneous classes.

Perimeter Challenge Lesson Plan

This lesson occurred at the beginning of the fifth week of a heterogeneous algebra class. Most of the students in the class were freshmen (ninth graders) coming from three different middle schools. There were a handful of sophomores and juniors who were repeating the class. Some of the students had documented learning disabilities.

Perimeter Challenges take place during days 5 and 6 of an 11-day unit that oriented students to a geometric representation of algebra, specifically a physical manipulative for numbers and variables (lab gear). We began the unit by introducing them to the lab gear pieces and helping them understand the similarities and differences between constants, variables and polynomials. On day 5, students were practicing combining like terms while working on groupworthy, perimeter puzzles.

I used the perimeter challenge warm-up to orient students to the task and get them thinking about $y - 5$ as a possible distance. Although students were exposed to both area and perimeter in middle school, they often confuse the two. This warm-up gave me an opportunity to define perimeter for them once again. The expression $y - 5$ is abstract for students. I have had students argue that it can also be $5 - y$ since y is a variable and can be a number smaller than 5. Alternatively, students may argue for a number value like 4.5 or a new variable like z. We discuss these possibilities as a whole class until consensus is reached. If the conversation stalls, I encourage the class to question and explore all answers for a few minutes in their groups and then bring their ideas to the whole class. I remind students that all answers may be correct but we need to reach consensus to move forward. If students lean towards 4.5 or z as a class, I share my desire to keep y a variable without adding more letters. If students argue for both $y - 5$ and $5 - y$, I first allow the discussion to play out without showing a preference for either. To encourage students to practice articulating their mathematical reasoning, I often ask students, "How do you know?" I want students to consider both as possible answers. This is a nice opportunity to redefine "smart" in a math classroom. Making sense of math from others' perspectives is part of that. If I again push for consensus, most students prefer $y - 5$. I encourage students who like $5 - y$ to use that if there is time to find an alternate answer.

Although the questions in the activity have not changed over the years, the structures and the task card have changed quite a bit. Originally, I gave each student a handout with all seven problems. I asked them to work together on the problems but did not structure the group work beyond that. I found that most students attempted the problems on their own and then tutored each other on the answers. I was surprised to find entire groups writing down the same incorrect answer. My initial assumption was that the problems were too hard. After closer inspection, I realized that the students had a fairly reasonable grasp of the mathematics. Still they were either making simple mistakes or changing their correct answers because a higher status student had a different answer. It struck me that they were having a breakdown in communication. I decided to create some structure to support both the task and the groupwork. I created the warm-up to familiarize them with the task. I used a multiple-abilities orientation to introduce the math skills that would help them during the task. Finally, I introduced norms and roles that would help them function as a group. Instead of giving them each a paper with all seven problems, I gave them one problem at a time. They received their points and the next problem only when the student I chose at random could justify the group's answer.

I face some unique challenges when I teach this lesson. I have to resist intervening in groups around mathematics unless it is absolutely necessary. Instead, I intervene around group behaviors. I will correct even the smallest group behavior. I will push a paper towards the middle if it's closer to one side of the table than another or I will ask a student to lean in or make better eye contact with his/her group members if I see body language that does not imply engagement. I am careful to give students clear and honest reasons for my intrusion and often apologize for interrupting their good work. When students call me over for a check in, I pick a student at random. I leave the impression that I come to the table with one question. In actuality, I will ask different questions depending on the student I pick. Perhaps I will ask a shy student to explain from the beginning. I may ask a more confident student a more pointed question that relates to the final answer. No matter how I start I insist every student give a complete explanation. It can be challenging to get to every group when they are ready. I often allow groups to move on and then quiz them on two problems at once later. Sometimes I do a quick check for correct answers and let them move on. Other times, I say, "You guys are having such great conversations, I don't even need to quiz you this time, but be ready next time." I cannot quiz each group thoroughly on every problem but if I quiz each group well twice, I am confident they are being held accountable and I am getting a glimpse into their understanding. I often end this lesson exhausted but thrilled that my students leave knowing they succeeded in solving some challenging math problems.

Groups finish day 1 with different and sometimes unique strategies for solving the perimeter problems. I want those strategies to become public at the beginning of day 2 so that students can have a larger "toolkit" when tackling these progressively more challenging problems. The second day's warm-up (see #1 of the LabGear and Perimeter warm-up student handout, which was featured in the film) is a fresh opportunity for students to practice and then present their strategies. I ask groups to build and then discuss the perimeter of the *Lab Gear man* (see Figure 3.5) in the middle of the table. I look for different strategies and ask students to present based on those strategies. I remind the class that the answer is only one small part of mathematics. Understanding the many unique methods that can bring you to an answer is the real meat. I push the class to question or rephrase the new strategies in each presentation and remind them that a successful math student often has several strategies in his/her "toolkit" to solve a problem.

I introduce part two of the perimeter challenge by highlighting the new ideas and strategies from the warm-up that will help them as they return to the problems from the day before. I encourage them to try the new strategies to deepen their understanding. These problems get progressively more challenging. I remind students of the norms and roles that will support their work (e.g., see overhead "Getting Good (Again) with Algebra Lab Gear") and remind them that I will again be holding them accountable with an explanation quiz.

Students get additional practice with perimeter and combining like terms by working on the Backwards Perimeter assignment. Again, students work in groups of four. It is a final opportunity for students to try strategies and solidify their understanding of perimeter and combining like terms. I hold groups accountable for each other's understanding with explanation quizzes or a participation quiz.

We have block scheduling, with hour-and-a-half-long periods. I usually spend two days to work on the perimeter challenges, and one day on the

Backwards Perimeter challenge (see Figure 3.7 at the end of this chapter). I do not expect students to finish the entire handout for Backwards Perimeter. Problems 1–4 are the core problems; the other problems are extra practice.

National Council of Teachers of Mathematics (NCTM) Standards Addressed

Algebra Standard for Grades 9–12

Represent and analyze mathematical situations and structures using algebraic symbols.

- understand the meaning of equivalent forms of expressions, equations, inequalities, and relations;
- use symbolic algebra to represent and explain mathematical relationships;
- judge the meaning, utility, and reasonableness of the results of symbol manipulations, including those carried out by technology.

Communication Standard for Grades 9–12

- organize and consolidate their mathematical thinking through communication;
- communicate their mathematical thinking coherently and clearly to peers, teachers, and others;
- analyze and evaluate the mathematical thinking and strategies of others;
- use the language of mathematics to express mathematical ideas precisely.

Problem Solving Standard for Grades 9–12

- build new mathematical knowledge through problem solving;
- solve problems that arise in mathematics and in other contexts;
- apply and adapt a variety of appropriate strategies to solve problems;
- monitor and reflect on the process of mathematical problem solving.

California Standards (CST) Addressed

Algebra Standards

Symbolic reasoning and calculations with symbols are central in algebra. Through the study of algebra, a student develops an understanding of the symbolic language of mathematics and the sciences. In addition, algebraic skills and concepts are developed and used in a wide variety of problem-solving situations.

10.0 Students add, subtract, multiply, and divide monomials and polynomials. Students solve multistep problems, including word problems, by using these techniques.

The Bigger Picture

The math department at San Lorenzo has been collaborating around curriculum and instruction for 20 years. I was fortunate to spend my first 12 years of teaching in that department. I owe my success to the group of amazing math teachers who have guided me, challenged me, and shared their successes and failures with me. The department has a shared vision of redefining "smart" for students in the math classroom and moving students to a more conceptual understanding of mathematics. We share instructional strategies and create curriculum together using this common vision.

Redefining "Smart" in a Math Classroom. We frame our work with a couple of guiding questions. How do we reduce our D/F grade rate in algebra? How do we change the definition of "smart" in a math classroom? The latter question is particularly challenging but essential to supporting all learners in a heterogeneous classroom. In general, students define their math intelligence through right and wrong answers: If I say the correct answer, I must understand math and I must be smart; when I get an answer wrong, I must not understand and I must not be as smart as I thought I was. Sharing answers, or even ideas, is a high-stakes endeavor for most math students. Sharing the wrong answer or idea threatens their confidence and their academic status with their peers. Students then resist sharing in a math classroom unless they are confident that they will say the correct answer. This thinking locks away a treasure trove of ideas, puts an unnecessary burden on the teacher to be the expert, and nearly paralyzes students when faced with difficult mathematics. In an attempt to protect students, teachers often teach procedure in place of conceptual understanding. Redefining "smart" math students as those who share ideas before they know they are correct and seek to understand different methods and representations is essential to creating a mathematics classroom space that values collaborative problem solving.

Moving from Procedural to Conceptual Algebra. Asking students to take risks in a procedural classroom, where teachers present the mathematical procedure for solving a problem and students practice the steps, will not work. You need to move from procedural to conceptual and create a curriculum that is challenging and rich. Telling students to redefine "smart" is only the beginning. They need to experience feeling smart as they take risks and work persistently. They will only believe they are smart at math when they succeed with challenging mathematics.

Instructional Strategies. Groupwork is just one of the many instructional strategies that we use to support our heterogeneous population of students. Whole-class discussion and pair work are also important in our classrooms. My colleagues and I share and discuss instructional strategies as we share new activities and new curriculum with each other.

Curriculum. We started working from College Preparatory Mathematics (CPM) but slowly rewrote and reorganized the curriculum to better fit our conceptual framework. Today we have a curriculum that was created in-house by teams of teachers who collaborated by subject area.

Day 5 of Unit

Detailed Lesson Plan: Perimeter Challenges

- Take out a piece of paper; put your name and title at the top.
- Get Lab Gear (see Figure 3.1).
- Place scratch paper in the middle of the table.
- Clear desks of everything else.

I. *Warm-up: Who's correct? How do you know?* (see Figures 3.2 and 3.3)

II. *Multiple Ability Orientation and Group Roles*

Multiple Ability Orientation (featured in the film)

Your group will do well if everyone . . .

- Takes risks and shares ideas: *"I'm not sure but I think . . ."*
- Listens to each other (don't just argue to win).
- Checks in with each other: *"Why don't you practice explaining to me before Ms. Evans comes?"*
- Asks group questions only.

You will be especially helpful if you . . .

- Can remember the names of the pieces.
- Can keep area and perimeter separate.
- Can recognize when a number should be used or when a variable should be used.
- Can keep track of the little details (include every side and not count sides twice).

Figure 3.1. Algebra Lab Gear Toolkit

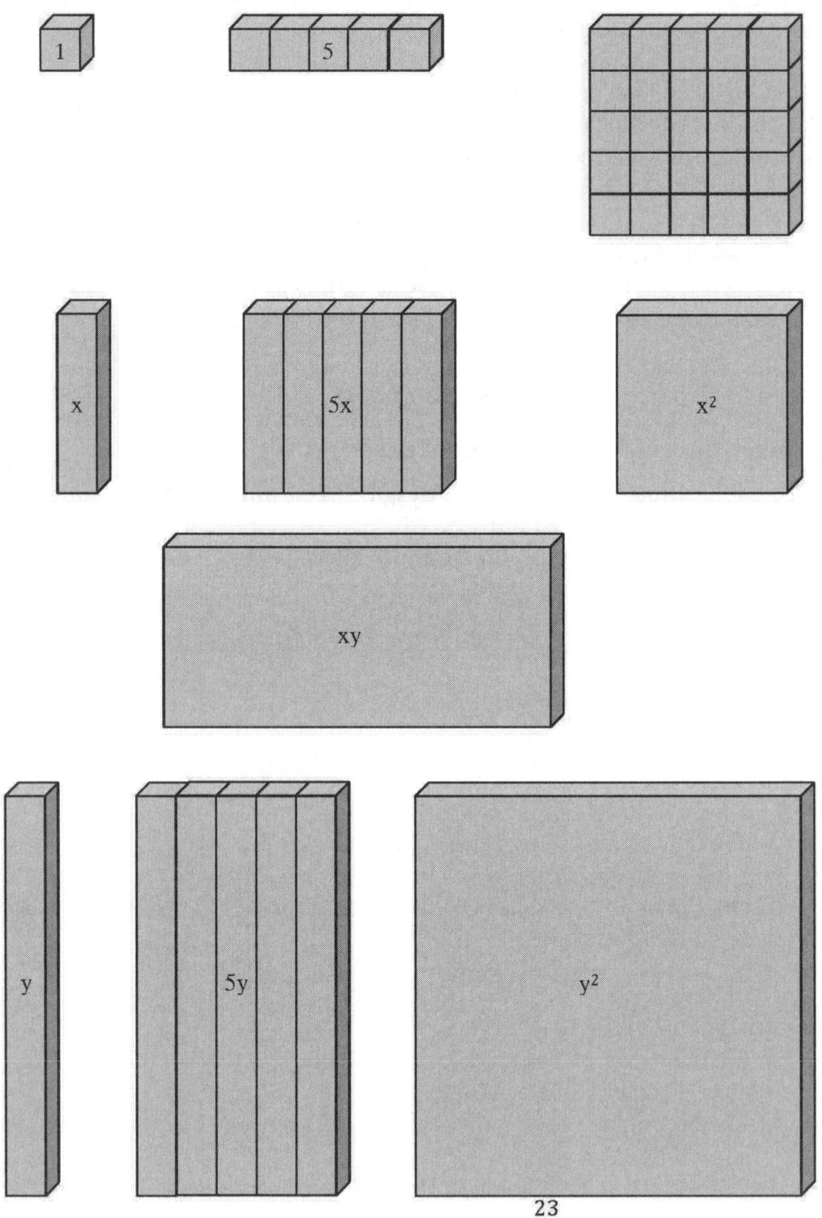

Figure 3.2. Who's Correct? How Do You Know?

- Build the following in the middle.
- Discuss the following with your group:

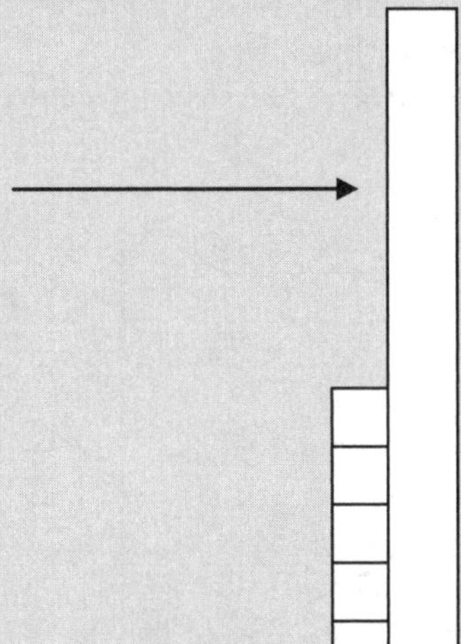

Who is correct? How do you know?
Why are the other ones incorrect?
What were they thinking?
Call your teacher over when everyone can explain!!!

Elizabeth said this length equals	Devon said this length equals	Marissa said this length equals
$y - 5$	$5 - y$	4.5

- Can combine like terms, including adding negative numbers correctly.
- Can find different methods for finding the perimeter and can explain them well.

Group Roles (featured in film)

TEAM CAPTAIN: Keep the group together and leaning in.
FACILITATOR: Check for understanding. Make sure every voice is heard. "What do you think?"
RESOURCE MANAGER: Make sure every problem is built in the middle and discussed before anyone writes on his/her own paper.
RECORDER REPORTER: Make sure work is correct on individual papers and everyone is prepared for a quiz.

Figure 3.3. Who's Correct? How Do You Know?

- Build the following in the middle.
- Discuss the following with your group:
  Who is correct? How do you know?
  Why are the other ones incorrect?
  What were they thinking?

Call your teacher over when everyone can explain!!!

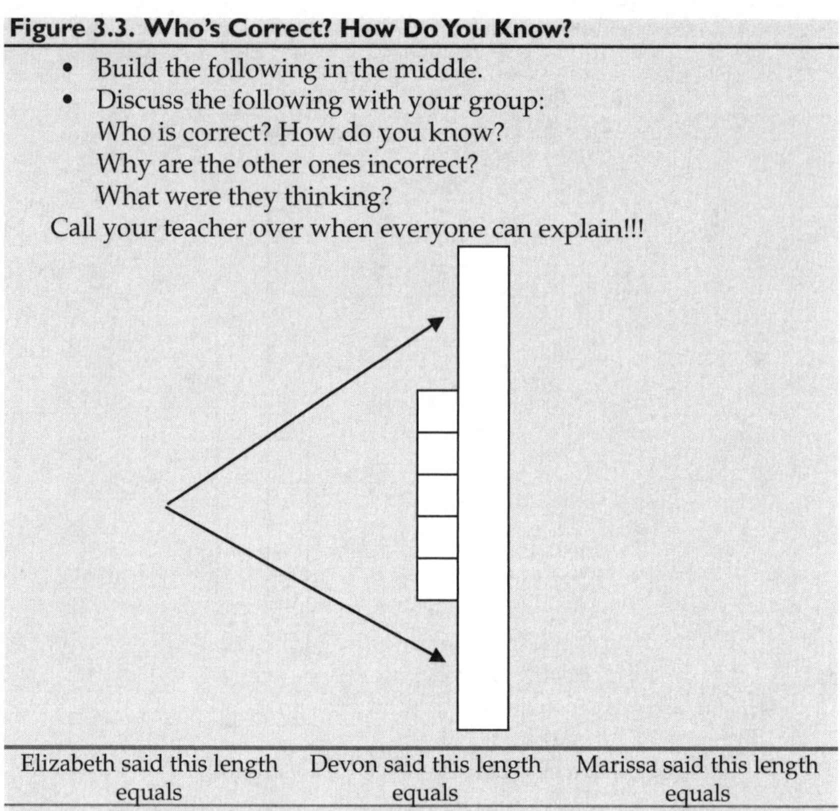

Elizabeth said this length equals	Devon said this length equals	Marissa said this length equals
$2y - 10$	$2y - 5$	$y - 5$

I will quiz you, and then give you a new challenge.

I. *Perimeter Challenges in small groups (see Figure 3.4).*

Day 6 of Unit

Detailed Lesson Plan: Perimeter Challenges Part 2

Warm-up:

- Clear desks of everything but a pencil.
- Place a piece of blank scratch paper in the middle of your table.
- Get Lab Gear.
- Resource Manager: Build the "Lab Gear Man" on the scratch paper in the middle of the table.

I'm looking for good body language and lots of questions and confirmations during your warm-up today. I'd like to hear:

"How should we start this?"
"I think maybe . . ."
"How did you get that? How do you know?"
"So what you're saying is . . ."
"Let me see if I can explain it."

Your question:
What is the perimeter of this lab gear man? (See Figure 3.5.) Call me over when your group has come to consensus and everyone can explain.

Activity:

Finish Perimeter Challenge.
Take out yesterday's paper.

We are doing more of the perimeter challenges that we started yesterday. You will need both good group behaviors and the new strategies you learned from the warm-up to be successful. Call me over after each for an explanation quiz and the next problem.

Remember:

TC:	Keep everyone involved.
F	What do you think? How do you know?
RM	Discussion in middle
RR	Have everyone show answer on own paper *after* the conversation is done. Prepare for the quiz.

See Figure 3.6 for more ideas on how to talk about group norms.

Figure 3.4. Perimeter Challenges

Problem #3 was featured in the film in the section on group quizzes.

I am looking for strong group work today. You will receive classwork points based on your group's responses when I quiz you. In order to make it through these, you will need to work together. Use your roles to help you.

Team Captain:	Keep the group together and leaning in.
Facilitator:	Check for understanding. Make sure every voice is heard. "What do you think?"
Resource Manager:	Make sure every problem is built in the middle and discussed before anyone writes on his/her own paper.
Recorder/ Reporter:	Work is correct on individual papers and group members are prepared for a quiz.

Figure 3.4. *continued*

Perimeter Challenge #1

1. Build this arrangement of Lab Gear blocks in the center of the table on scratch paper.
2. Discuss how to find its perimeter. Make sure everyone understands and agrees as you go.
3. Sketch it on your own paper.
4. Write in each side length and the final perimeter answer on your own paper.

When every person in your group can explain how you arrived at your answer, call me over to get your next challenge.

Perimeter Challenge #2

1. Build this arrangement of Lab Gear blocks[1] in the center of the table on scratch paper.
2. Discuss how to find its perimeter. Make sure everyone understands and agrees as you go.
3. Sketch it on your own paper.
4. Write in each side length and the final perimeter answer on your own paper.

When every person in your group can explain how you arrived at your answer, call me over to get your next challenge.

Figure 3.4. *continued*

Perimeter Challenge #3

1. Build this arrangement of Lab Gear blocks[2] in the center of the table on scratch paper.
2. Discuss how to find its perimeter. Make sure everyone understands and agrees as you go.
3. Sketch it on your own paper.
4. Write in each side length and the final perimeter answer on your own paper.

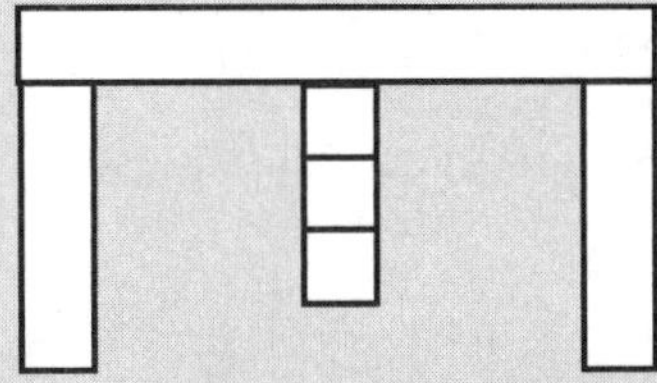

When every person in your group can explain how you arrived at your answer, call me over to get your next challenge.

Perimeter Challenge #4

1. Build this arrangement of Lab Gear blocks[3] in the center of the table on scratch paper.
2. Discuss how to find its perimeter. Make sure everyone understands and agrees as you go.
3. Sketch it on your own paper.
4. Write in each side length and the final perimeter answer on your own paper.

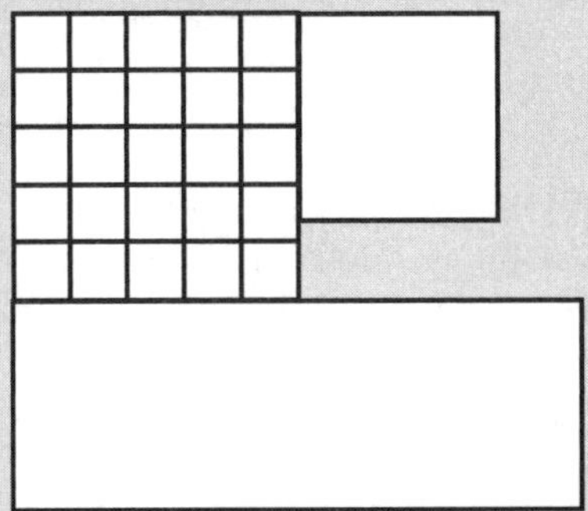

When every person in your group can explain how you arrived at your answer, call me over to get your next challenge.

Figure 3.4. *continued*

Perimeter Challenge #5

1. Using the blocks pictured below, build an arrangement for each of these perimeters.

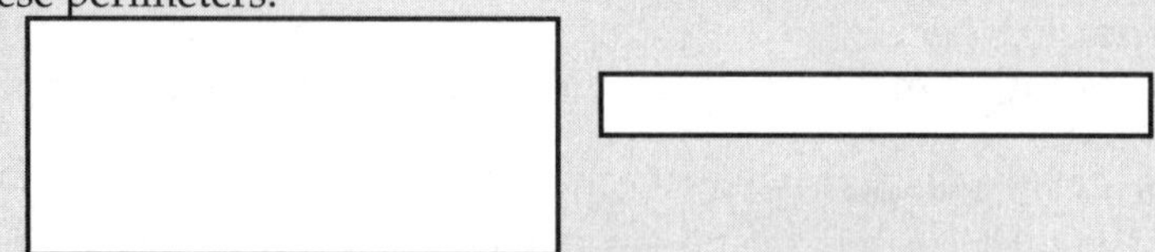

2. Work on it in the middle of the table first. Make sure everyone understands and agrees as you go.
3. Sketch it on your own paper.
4. Write in each side length to show your arrangement is correct.

Your perimeters are:[4]

a) $2y + 2x + 4$ b) $2x + 4y$ c) $4y + 4$

When every person in your group can explain how you arrived at your answer, call me over to get your next challenge.

Perimeter Challenge #6

Arrange any four blocks so that the perimeter of the resulting figure[5] is:

$$2x + 2y + 4$$

How many different solutions can you find?

When every person in your group can explain how you arrived at your answer, call me over to get your next challenge.

Perimeter Challenge #7

Arrange any three blocks so that the perimeter of the resulting figure is:

$$2x + 4$$

How many different solutions can you find?

When every person in your group can explain how you arrived at your answer, call me over to get your next challenge.

Notes to Figure 3.4

1 Henri Picciotto (1995). *Lab Gear Activities for Algebra 1*. Chicago: Creative Publications, p. 23.

2 Ibid. (figure looks like E in Picciotto's book).

3 Ibid.

4 Ibid.

5 Ibid., p. 2.

Figure 3.5. Lab Gear and Perimeter Warm-up

(Problem 1 was featured in the film in the section on Multiple Abilities)

1. Build this shape with your partner. Find the perimeter of this shape together. Simplify your answer. Make sure you both agree and can explain.

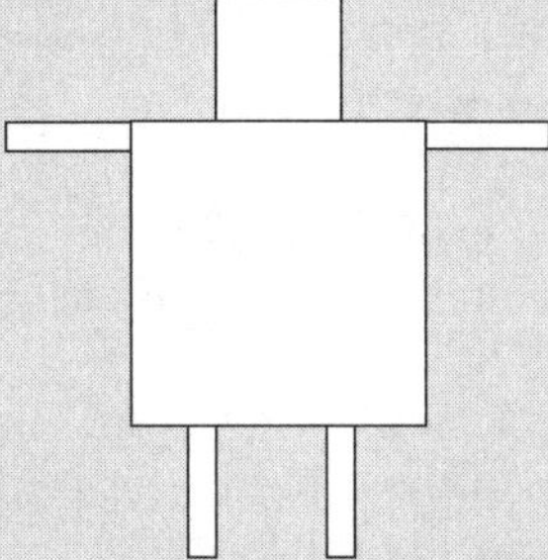

2. If $y = 10$ and $x = 4$ in the shape above, what would its perimeter be? Show or explain how you got your answer.

Find what is missing in each of these equal expressions.

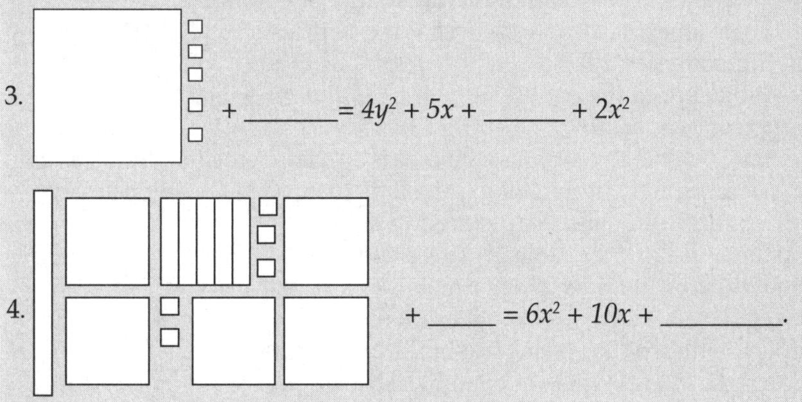

3. + ______ $= 4y^2 + 5x +$ ______ $+ 2x^2$

4. + ______ $= 6x^2 + 10x +$ ________.

Figure 3.6. Getting Good (Again) with Algebra Lab Gear

If you're thinking:	*Your group needs you to:*
"Hey, I know this!"	▶Be patient ▶Explain slowly ▶Give reasons!—Tell how you know! ▶Let others handle the Lab Gear ("hands-off") ▶Take your time, and demand that your group stays together.
"What the heck is this?"	▶Ask questions ▶Be "hands-on" with the Lab Gear ▶Take your time, and demand your group stays with you

Figure 3.7. Additional Resources—Backwards Perimeter

(Problem 1c was featured in the film during the section on Assigning Competence)

These are trickier than they look. You will need your group members to succeed. Remember to follow these steps when doing each problem:

- Put the pieces in the middle of the table on scratch paper.
- Make sure everyone is ready and leaning in.
- Discuss how to answer the problem. Take risks. Say what you think even before you know it's correct.
- Make sure everyone understands the answer and can explain it.
- Show the answer on your own paper.
-

1. Using exactly the blocks to the right, build an arrangement for each of these perimeters with your group in the middle of the table.

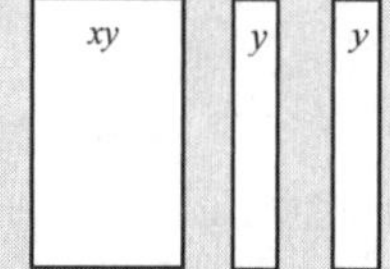

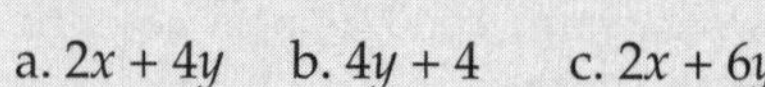

a. $2x + 4y$ b. $4y + 4$ c. $2x + 6y$

Once everyone agrees, sketch each answer on your paper.

2. Build the figure at the right in the middle of your table.
   a. Write an expression to represent the perimeter of this shape.
   b. What would the perimeter be if $x = 3$ and $y = 5$ *(show your work).*

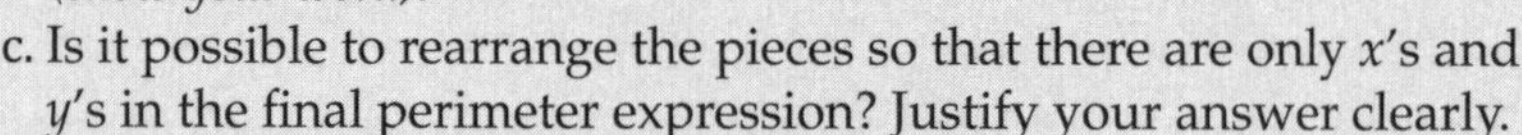

   c. Is it possible to rearrange the pieces so that there are only x's and y's in the final perimeter expression? Justify your answer clearly.

3. Place the tiles $2x$ and $2y$ (pictured to the right) in the middle of the table. Arrange them so that they would have the perimeter $4x + 2y$. Sketch the arrangement on your own paper.

4. Use the tiles xy, $2y$, x, and 1 to build the shape to the right in the middle of the table. Discuss its perimeter with your group.

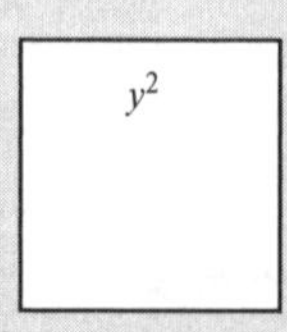

Write an expression that represents the perimeter.

Now rearrange the pieces so that the perimeter becomes $4y + 4x + 2$. Sketch your answer below.

5. Arrange any three blocks so that the perimeter of the figure is $4x + 4$.* Sketch your answer. Can you use any three blocks? Explain.
6. The perimeter of the shape at right is 32 units. Find possible values for x and y. Is there more than one possible solution? If so, find another solution. If not, explain how you know there is only one solution.

*Picciota, 1995, p. 23.

CHAPTER 4

The New Swimming Pool

Maika Watanabe, Angela Knotts, and Jon Deane

The New Swimming Pool lesson occurred in March, midway into the second semester of a heterogeneous ninth-grade mathematics class designed to cover California content standards for both Algebra 1 and Geometry. At that time, ninth graders at Summit Prep took a double block of math (two consecutive class periods) each day in order to allow time to cover both sets of standards.

This lesson took place towards the end of a 5-week unit on area, volume, and the Pythagorean Theorem developed by the Interactive Mathematics Program (IMP) and titled, "Do Bees Build It Best?" The unit question examines whether the honeycomb is the most efficient shape for storing honey. Prior to the Problem of the Week (POW), students had worked with Geoboards to further their understanding about area, worked with the Pythagorean Theorem, and explored the volumes of prisms. They had also completed a similar activity in class entitled, "More Fencing, Bigger Corrals" from the IMP curricula, in which students were asked to build the "best" corral in terms of maximizing area given different amounts of fencing. Initially the students needed to find the dimensions of a rectangular corral that resulted in the most area; then, since rectangles are "boring," they were asked to maximize the area of corrals shaped like other polygons (triangles, quadrilaterals, pentagons, etc.). The New Swimming Pool was a spin-off on the corral problem, now looking into volume.

Students spent one hour in class working on this problem in groups, drawing their group answer on butcher paper. We taped the posters up around the classroom walls, and students did a gallery walk, where students walk individually around to the different posters, reading the various groups' solutions to the swimming pool problem. As teachers, we then facilitated a discussion on the similarities and differences in various groups' responses to the same problem. Students then spent about a half hour writing up their individual responses; they were allowed to consult with each other as they worked on these individual responses. They then finished the write-up over two nights of homework.

This assignment was open-ended, since we did not tell them what "best" was. There were no "right" answers, particularly for the fifth question or the challenge question. Students had to meet the requirements specified and justify their design. For example, in coming up with designs for swimming pools, students discussed how a swimming pool with a 3-foot-deep section that suddenly dropped straight down to 10 feet was not a child-friendly design. In working on this problem, students practiced calculating the volumes for rectangular and trapezoidal-shaped prisms and saw how this content was related to the real world.

Challenges in Teaching This Lesson

The biggest challenge in teaching this lesson is making sure that you have consistent norms structured for groups so that when you have a word like "best" in the problem, students know how to engage in a discussion.

To reinforce group norms, we stated at the beginning of a task what we were looking for (e.g., all leaning in, equal voices, listening and contributing respectfully, asking questions, making others explain and justify their ideas with math reasons), expectations with which all students were very familiar by this point in the year. During the task, we listened to students talk and made notes about our observations in the form of a "participation quiz," as featured in the DVD. The culture of the school came in big time here—in all of students' classes, we often discussed the six Core Characteristics (Respect, Responsibility, Courage, Curiosity, Compassion, and Integrity), so these norms were getting reinforced in a lot of places. We tried to bring the six Core Characteristics up and work them into our expectations for how they worked together. When the task was over, we also gave them more specific feedback about their social behavior and group interactions, both by praising individuals for good work and by pointing out opportunities for continued improvement in the class overall.

We also used group roles (Team Captain, Resource Manager/Time Keeper, Recorder/Reporter, Facilitator) to give everyone in the group some responsibility for how the group functioned, and tried to train them in what jobs each role was responsible for doing. To be honest, training students to take on these roles and perform them consistently and well takes years of coaching and practice; it can also be difficult for teachers to stay attuned to how students fulfill these roles, which is something we are still working on. One thing that helped was providing specific language students can use—we even typed phrases out and handed them out for kids to keep at their tables ("I'm not sure what you meant by . . ." "Could you explain that again in a different way?" "I think what you're saying is . . ." "I understand what you're saying, but I wonder about . . ." "I have some questions about . . ." etc.).

These days the math department has developed something they call "Powerful Math Learner" (PML) behaviors. Beginning with the 2010 4-week summer math program in which about 60% of the Class of 2014 participated, we taught the students that they would be successful in their Summit mathematics courses if they consistently practiced three key behaviors of Powerful Math Learners: taking risks, contributing productively, and working persistently. We evaluated each student on all three every day, provided them with written, personalized feedback at the end of each week, and sometimes devoted an entire day to focusing specifically on one PML. At the end of a day, week, or activity, we tried to wrap up by giving examples from our notes of specific instances of when a student displayed one of the PMLs and helped move the group forward with the problem as a result. Not only did this help reinforce the PMLs and assure the students that we noticed how they interacted with one another, but because the PMLs are behaviors that students can *choose* to engage in (rather than knowledge or skills that they may or may not have), it also gave us an opportunity to assign Powerful Math Learner status to students who may be traditionally seen by the peers as having low academic status due to poor academic preparation.

Assessments

Students completed individual write-ups after they worked on their group poster. The rubric we used to assess their individual write-ups is included in Table 4.1.

National Council of Teachers of Mathematics (NCTM) Standards Addressed

Geometry Standard for Grades 9–12

Use visualization, spatial reasoning, and geometric modeling to solve problems

- draw and construct representations of two- and three-dimensional geometric objects using a variety of tools;
- visualize three-dimensional objects and spaces from different perspectives and analyze their cross sections;
- use geometric ideas to solve problems in, and gain insights into, other disciplines and other areas of interest such as art and architecture.

Communication Standard for Grades 9–12

- organize and consolidate their mathematical thinking through communication;

- communicate their mathematical thinking coherently and clearly to peers, teachers, and others;
- analyze and evaluate the mathematical thinking and strategies of others;
- use the language of mathematics to express mathematical ideas precisely.

Problem-Solving Standard for Grades 9–12

- build new mathematical knowledge through problem solving;
- solve problems that arise in mathematics and in other contexts;
- apply and adapt a variety of appropriate strategies to solve problems;
- monitor and reflect on the process of mathematical problem solving.

California Standards (CST) Addressed

Geometry Standards

8.0 Students know, derive, and solve problems involving the perimeter, circumference, area, volume, lateral area, and surface area of common geometric figures.

9.0 Students compute the volumes and surface areas of prisms, pyramids, cylinders, cones, and spheres; and students commit to memory the formulas for prisms, pyramids, and cylinders.

11.0 Students determine how changes in dimensions affect the perimeter, area, and volume of common geometric figures and solids.

The New Swimming Pool Problem of the Week

The Clotts family is planning to build a swimming pool in their backyard. Their backyard is long and narrow, with dimensions of 150 feet by 40 feet. They live on top of a small hill, so the town building department says that they can build a pool which holds no more than 10,000 cubic feet of water. (In case there is an earthquake that ruptures the pool, the town does not want the whole neighborhood to be flooded.) The family wants the largest pool possible that meets all of their needs. Mrs. Clotts wants to be sure that there is at least 5 feet of pool deck around all the sides of the pool. The younger kids in the family want to have a shallow end to play in that is 3 feet deep. The older kids want a deep end that is 10 feet deep for diving. Mr. Clotts wants the pool to be at least 50 feet long so that he does not get dizzy when he swims laps. The whole family wants the pool to be at least 15 feet wide so that it will be fun for playing Marco Polo.

To keep building costs down and to make it easier to have an automatic pool cover, the surface of the pool needs to be a rectangle. The pool company wants all the dimensions of the pool to be in whole numbers for ease of construction planning.

YOUR ULTIMATE TASK: What should be the dimensions of the best pool for the Clotts family?

BEFORE you answer that question, answer these questions. Include all of your results in your write-up.

1. What would be the largest pool which could be built if the whole pool had a depth of 3 feet?

   (Sorry—no diving allowed!)

2. What would be the largest pool which could be built if the whole pool had a depth of 10 feet?

   (Must past a swimming test to use the pool!)

The pool company says they can build a pool with a 3-foot shallow end and a 10-foot deep end two different ways. They can build a shallow end of 3 feet and then have a drop-off down to 10 feet so that the bottom of the pool has two levels. The drop-off edge would be perpendicular to the side of the pool. Or they can build a pool with a bottom that slopes from 3 feet to 10 feet.

3. What would be the best dimensions for a pool with a 3-foot-deep part and a 10-foot-deep part?
4. What would be the best dimensions for a pool with a bottom which slopes from 3 to 10 feet?
5. Which pool best meets all the needs of the family?

*6. Challenge: Now all the neighbors are thinking about how nice it would be to have a pool. They have yards of many different sizes, but they all have the same requirement—10,000 cubic feet or less. How would you build the best pool which will work for any yard?

Write-up

Due Friday 3/23!

1. Problem statement: Summarize the problem. In mathematical terms, what are you looking for to solve the problem?

Table 4.1 Rubric for Individual Write-Ups

Paper Element	Revise	Acceptable (70–80%)	Good (80–90%)	Great! (90–100%)	Score
Formatting & Professionalism	☐ Missing name, date, class, or title ☐ Difficult to follow/understand due to neatness/organization ☐ One or more sections are missing	☐ Name, date, class, & title included ☐ Most of the product is reasonably neat, well-organized, and legible; could be improved ☐ All three sections are addressed	☐ Name, date, class, & title included ☐ Nearly all of the product is neat, well-organized, and legible; typed where possible ☐ All three sections are thoroughly addressed	☐ Name, date, class, & title included ☐ Product is so neat, well-organized, and easy to follow that it is almost professional; typed where possible ☐ All three sections (introduction, body, & reflection) are fully addressed	____/5
Problem Statement	☐ It is unclear what problem is to be solved ☐ None or almost none of the important information is included	☐ Describes some important aspects of the problem, but the description could be clearer ☐ Important information is left out, OR a lot of irrelevant information is included	☐ Clearly summarizes the problem in the author's own words ☐ All relevant information is included ☐ May include some information that is not relevant to solving the problem	☐ Clearly & concisely summarizes the problem in the author's own words ☐ All the relevant information is included	____/5
Mathematics—Solutions & Process	☐ Most solutions are incorrect or missing ☐ Most tasks do not include sufficient work ☐ Little or no evidence to support statements ☐ Most explanations are too confusing to follow/understand	☐ Mostly correct and complete solutions are given to most tasks; several errors ☐ More work is needed in several spots ☐ Many statements need more EVIDENCE ☐ Some explanations are difficult to follow / understand	☐ Correct and complete solutions for most parts of the problem; some minor errors ☐ Sufficient work is shown to support most solutions ☐ Most mathematical statements are supported by EVIDENCE ☐ Explanations are mostly clear, concise, and easy to follow	☐ Correct and complete solutions for ALL parts of the problem ☐ Sufficient work is shown to support the solutions ☐ All mathematical statements are supported by EVIDENCE ("Because" statements) ☐ Explanations are clear, concise, and easy to follow	____/15

Technical Writing Tools	☐ Few or no tech writing tools -OR- Most tech writing tools . . . ☐ Don’t support the solution ☐ Are messy ☐ Are confusing ☐ Are not labeled	☐ Some diagrams, equations, graphs, and tables; more are needed Tech writing tools are included, but several of them . . . ☐ Don’t support the solution ☐ Are messy ☐ Are confusing ☐ Are not labeled	☐ Lots of diagrams, equations, graphs, and tables, but more might help ☐ Some effort to embed tech writing tools in the paper electronically Most tech writing tools . . . ☐ Support the solution ☐ Are neat & well-organized ☐ Are labeled ☐ Are easy to read / understand	☐ A wealth of diagrams, equations, graphs, and tables support and explain solutions! All tech writing tools . . . ☐ Support the solution ☐ Are neat & well-organized ☐ Are labeled ☐ Are easy to read / understand	____/10
Evaluation & Self-Assessment	☐ Several questions are not answered	☐ Thoughtful & insightful answers to most reflection questions, -OR- ☐ Superficial answers to all questions	☐ Thoughtful answers to all reflection questions	☐ Thoughtful & insightful answers to all reflection questions	____/5

2. Process: Explain the work you did and the methods and formulas you used to find your answers. Be sure to show or attach some of your work!
3. Solution: What pool dimensions did you decide are best for the family? Why?
4. Evaluation: Was this POW too hard, too easy, just right, worthwhile, etc.? How did this problem relate to the math we have been doing? What did you learn from it?
5. Self-Assessment: How did your actions contribute to making your group productive? Did you contribute to a pleasant working environment (i.e., were you helpful and supportive)? How did you contribute to finding the solution?

CHAPTER 5

Understanding Phenomena Through Intermolecular Forces

The science of soap, capillary action, fats, boiling points, cell science, and proteins

Howard Shen

This project occurred about halfway through the second semester of a tenth-grade General Chemistry class, at the end of my unit about bonding. By this point in the year, students had already had one unit focused on phases of matter and phase changes, and a unit focused on atomic structure and the periodic table. My units in my first year of teaching were long, about half a semester each. Following this project was my unit on reactions, which included stoichiometry, kinetics, equilibrium, and acids and bases.

Teacher to Teacher

This is the project where I learned how critical it is for a groupworthy task to not have a "right answer." In this case, I stressed that I did not care if the students actually determined the actual scientifically accurate answer to their prompt. Instead, I wanted to see how students applied their knowledge of bonding and intermolecular forces to a new situation (see Figure 5.1). This opened up the possibility for students to take academic risks and to think critically instead of going to look up the answers online. What students thought of as "ridiculous" explanations would often prove to be on the right track, and students were excited about these realizations.

I also underestimated the difficulty of the project for the students based on prior content knowledge. Below is the order in which I would rank the complexity of the projects, from easiest to hardest:

1. The Science of Soap
2. Capillary Action
3. Fats
4. Boiling Points
5. Cell Science (Cell Membranes)
6. Proteins

If your students have NOT had biology, cell science is very difficult—coming up with a membrane structure makes very little sense if you do not understand cell structure. Boiling points can be easier or harder based on the molecules you put on the page; it also is the project that most noticeably becomes less challenging with scaffolding. In later years, I included a homework assignment that gave students more background information, and I also broke down steps for some projects through starter questions (see Figures 5.2 and 5.3).

The individual write-up is necessary to encourage students who are not outwardly curious to pay attention to the group answer. In addition, rather than just asking for a summary of the group answer to the original task card question(s), the individual write-up question requires students to demonstrate their understanding of intermolecular forces by extending the concepts from their project to a new, but very closely related question on an individual assessment. The project task card includes questions I have used for the individual write-ups.

I have had varying degrees of success with the quality of group presentations and this is something I continue to work on. Some ideas might be to go over the rubric carefully with students (see Table 5.1), to show examples of effective and ineffective visuals, and to encourage students to self-assess their group product using the rubric before the presentations.

Lesson Plan

Before project: Discuss polarity, the structure of water. I had students do plates 6, 11, 16, 30, and 32 from Griffin (1986).[1]

Day 1. [We were finishing up a prior unit, so only used the last 30 minutes of class time on the new project.]

10 minutes: Explain project to groups. Emphasize that the point is not to get the "right" answer, but to make use of your knowledge of bonding and intermolecular forces.

5 minutes: Groups select projects at random (draw papers from a hat).

5 minutes: Discuss line notation for organic compounds (not drawing the Cs and Hs in an organic compound). (Pentane molecular structure and line structures included.)

Assign homework

Remaining time: Groups begin work on projects.

Days 2 and 3. Groups work on projects.

Day 4. Each group presents its project. A graphic organizer encourages all students to listen and take notes.

[1]Griffin, R. D. (1986). *Biology Coloring Book.* New York: Collins Reference.

Figure 5.1. Project Description

When: Work time in class on 4/14–4/16
Presentations in class: 4/17
Individual Write-up and Evaluations Due: 4/20

Who: First, you will work with your group.
Second, you will do an individual part.

How: You should be able to address your topic through an understanding of intermolecular forces and bonding. This may require that you spend time reviewing intermolecular forces and bonding before you begin working on your topic. You are not allowed to look up the answer to any part using an outside resource.

What: The first part of the project is the groupwork portion. You will work with your group in class on Tuesday, Wednesday, and Thursday. On Friday you will give a group presentation about your topic. Each group has a different topic.
In your presentation, you should discuss these things:

- Describe very briefly what your topic is (Ex: What is a cell membrane? What's special about it?).
- What are some important non-chemistry facts or ideas that affect the chemistry of the topic? (Ex: Cells float in water and are filled with water, or kinetic energy is mass times velocity squared.)
- What ideas are vital to review with the class? (Ex: The bigger the molecule, the stronger the London dispersion force, or London dispersion forces require molecules to be close to each other to be effective.)
- Discuss the answer to the primary question in your task. Include an explanation of the chemistry (bonding and intermolecular forces) that dictates or controls what happens.

Your presentation should have some sort of useful visual.

The second part of the project is the individual portion. This will consist of a brief response to a question about the topics. This response may be written, drawn, videotaped, or some combination thereof. Your response should include evidence based on the bonding and/or intermolecular forces present in the system described.

Choose *one* of the six to answer:

1. Why do heptane [C_7H_{16}] and water have almost identical boiling points

Figure 5.1 *continued*

2. Why does sodium laurate (a major ingredient of soap) dissolve in water, but calcium laurate (soap scum) does not?

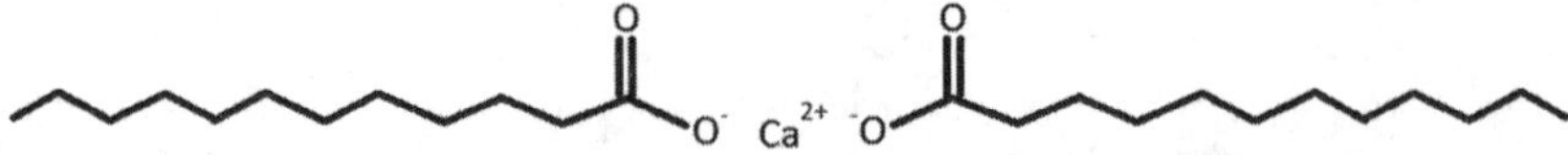

3. Will a trans fat behave more like a saturated fat or a cis unsaturated fat? Why? How does this explain the recent fuss about trans fats?
4. In sickle cell anemia (a genetic disease), a protein in blood folds into long fibers instead of folding into a sphere, because a valine amino acid replaces a glutamate amino acid in a protein. Why does this change the protein folding so drastically?
5. Rate the following based on how much they will display capillary action: acetaldehyde, acetic acid, ethanol. Explain why you ranked them the way you did.

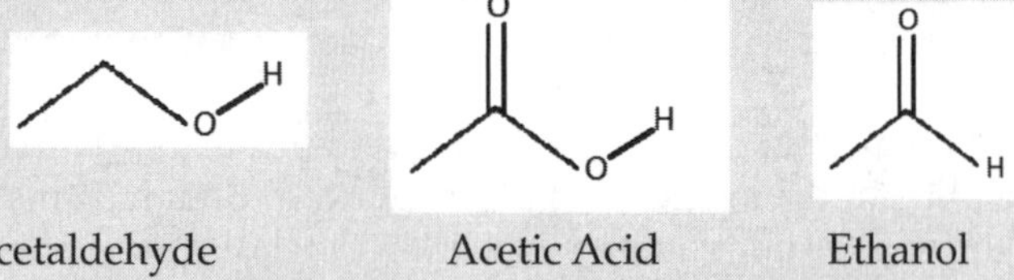

Acetaldehyde Acetic Acid Ethanol

6. Why is it difficult for H_3O+ to diffuse through the cell membrane, but C_6H_6 diffuses through the cell membrane easily?

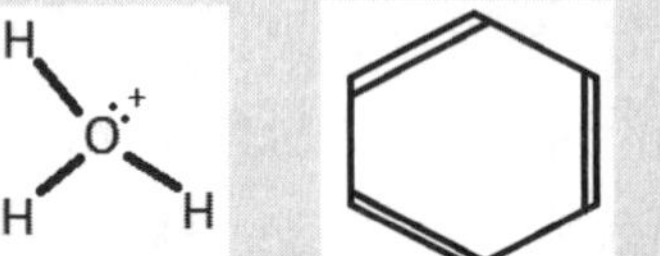

You may choose any of the 6 to answer, though I do recommend that you pick the one related to your group's topic.

Lastly, you will need to submit a group evaluation and a self-evaluation. Detach the rubric from the packet. Evaluate your group presentation, groupwork, and individual answer based on the rubric, highlighting how you think you performed on each part.

Standards

California, Science Standards, Chemistry

Standard 2: Biological, chemical, and physical properties of matter result from the ability of atoms to form bonds from electrostatic forces between electrons and protons and between atoms and molecules. As a basis for understanding this concept:

a. *Students know* atoms combine to form molecules by sharing electrons to form covalent or metallic bonds or by exchanging electrons to form ionic bonds.

d. *Students know* the atoms and molecules in liquids move in a random pattern relative to one another because the intermolecular forces are too weak to hold the atoms or molecules in a solid form.

h. *Students know* how to identify solids and liquids held together by Van der Waals forces or hydrogen bonding and relate these forces to volatility and boiling/melting point temperatures.

Figure 5.2. Task Cards

The Science of Soap Task Card

Background Questions

1. What happens to the individual ions when an ionic substance dissolves?
2. Why are the water molecules attracted to the ions?
3. What types of common substances are difficult to wash off with only water?

Background Information

The typical soap particle looks like:

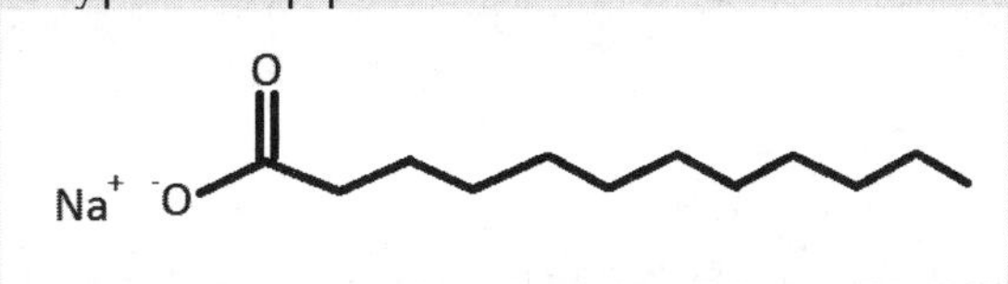

Most greases and oils (the substances that are difficult to wash off) are lipids.

Figure 5.2 *continued*

Your task:

Some starter questions:

1. Why are salt and sugar soluble in water? (Look up the structure of sugar in Monday's packet.)
2. Why aren't lipids soluble in water?
3. Which side of the dissolved soap molecule would be attracted to water? Which side would interact well with the lipids?
4. How could a lot of soap molecules come together to attract one lipid molecule?

Main question: Use your knowledge of intermolecular forces and bonding to create plausible explanations for the following question:

How does soap make lipids dissolve in water?

For the individual portion, you will need to know a little bit about soap scum, which is soap reacted with calcium (see structure below).

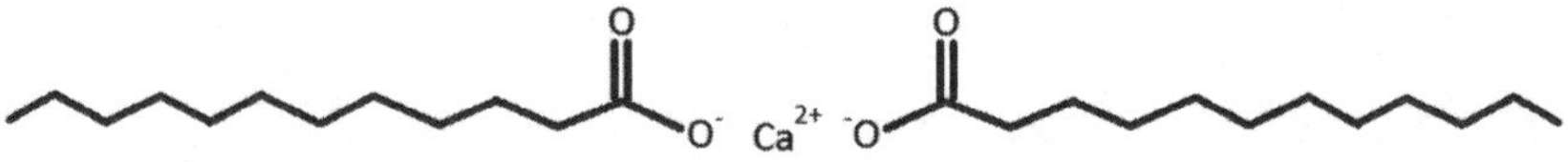

O O
O^- Ca^{2+} ^-O

Soap scum is a white residue left behind if you have hard water. Soap scum is not soluble in water.

Capillary Action Task Card

Background Information

If you stick one corner or one edge of a piece of paper in water, the water will gradually crawl up the paper until a large section of the paper is wet. This is called capillary action or the capillary effect. Try it!

Paper is made from cellulose, which was described in your packet from Monday.

Your task:

Starter questions:

1. What force needs to be overcome to draw the water up?
2. How will water interact with cellulose?

Main question: What causes the capillary effect?

Figure 5.2 *continued*

Fats! Task Card

Background Questions

1. What are the two major kinds of fat you find in food?
2. Which kind of fat is unhealthier?
3. What are the health risks associated with a high-fat diet?

Background Information

Make sure you read the Lipid handout you have/had for homework (Plate 17).

Saturated fats are unhealthier because they are more likely to be solid at room temperature, while unsaturated fats are more likely to be liquid at room temperature. For example, butter is mostly saturated fat, while olive oil is mostly unsaturated fat.

Most natural unsaturated fats have cis double bonds.

Your task:

Starter questions:

1. Which sections of a fat molecule are polar? Which are nonpolar? Which one is bigger?
2. Based on your answer to #1, which intermolecular force is the most important in fats?
3. What are some ways to make that intermolecular force more effective?
4. Based on the background info, are intermolecular forces stronger in unsaturated fats or saturated fats?
5. How does the shape of the fat affect the intermolecular forces?

Main question: Why are unsaturated fats more likely to be solid at room temperature than unsaturated fats?

Boiling Points Task Card

Background Information

Different substances have different boiling points.

Make sure to review your notes about phase changes! (Big Ideas: Matter, March 30)

Keep in mind the relationship of temperature and kinetic energy, as well as the relationship of kinetic energy, mass of a particle, and velocity of a particle.

Figure 5.2 *continued*

Task

Main question: How will the boiling points of these substances compare? (Rank them from lowest to highest boiling point.) Provide evidence for your choices.

Ammonia 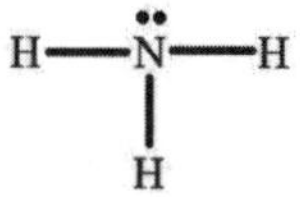	Water 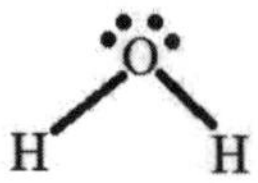	Acetone 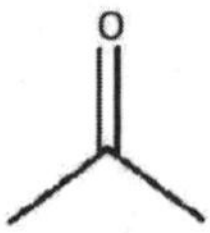
Methanol 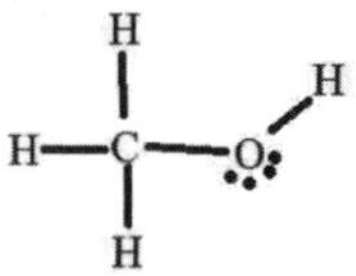	Methyl ether 	Acetic acid 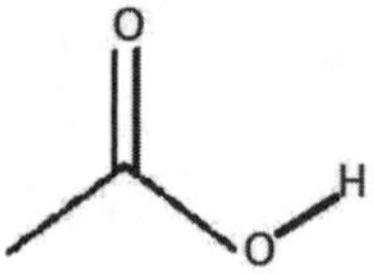
Nitrogen 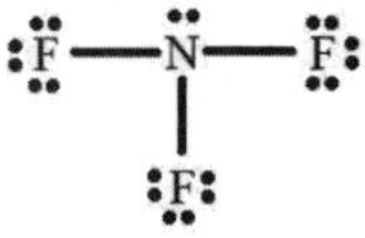 trifluoride	Hexane 	Dihydrogen sulfide 
Methane 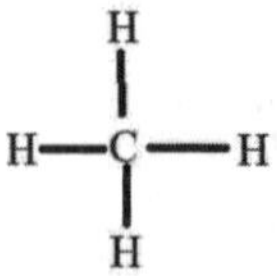	Chloromethane 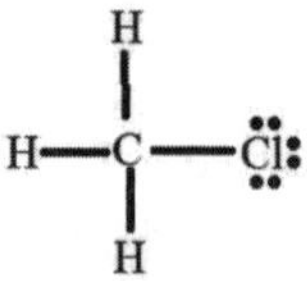	Ethanol 
Formaldehyde 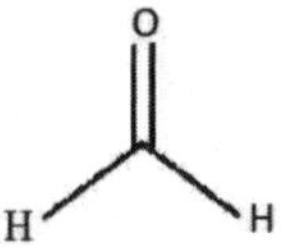	Hydrogen chloride 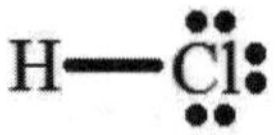	Fluorine 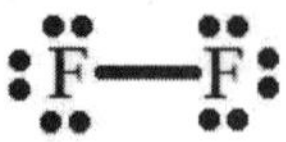

Figure 5.2 *continued*

Cell Science Task Card

Background Information

The cell is filled with cytoplasm. Cytoplasm is mostly made up of water. Additionally, the substance outside the cell is also made up of mostly water.

The cell maintains a very strict balance of many things, such as sugars, proteins, and ions. The cell membrane is responsible for maintaining this balance. Often, concentrations of substances inside and outside the cell are very uneven. The cell membrane must be designed to allow some substances to travel freely back and forth but prevent other substances from doing the same thing. This is called *selective permeability.*

The basic molecule of the cell membrane looks like this:

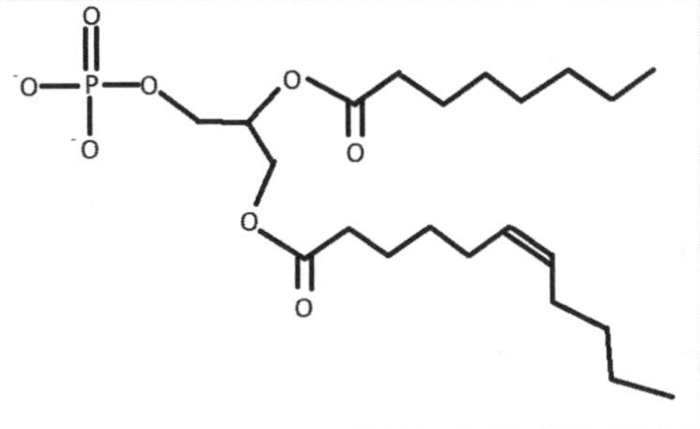

Your task:

Starter questions:

1. How would these molecules interact with a single water molecule?
2. If there were a few of these molecules surrounded by water, how would the molecules come together? Keep in mind how the membrane molecules interact with water molecules.
3. How could you form a barrier between two bodies of water using the membrane molecules?
4. If you have a barrier, what types of particles will be able to travel across the membrane? (Try drawing your membrane, thinking about which intermolecular forces are in action. Don't forget about the water on either side of the membrane, and what intermolecular forces they are exerting!)

Main question: How do millions of these molecules come together to form a cell membrane? How does this cause the cell membrane to be selectively permeable?

Figure 5.2 *continued*

Proteins Task Card

Background Information

Make sure you've read Plate 30 that you have/had for homework. Plate 30 is from Griffin (1986).

Proteins are made in the ribosomes, which are in the cell. They are surrounded by cytoplasm. Cytoplasm is mostly made up of water.

The functionality of a protein is totally dependent on its shape. The amino acid chain folds into a very specific shape. If the shape is altered, then the protein either doesn't function or functions in a totally unexpected way.

Your task:

Starter question:

1. How do the side groups on different amino acids interact differently with water?
2. Which side groups "want" to be in water? Which don't?
3. If a long chain of amino acids is surrounded by water, how do the side groups affect which way each amino acid is pulled?

Main question: How does a protein (a long chain of amino acids) "know" what shape to fold into?

Figure 5.3. Homework Questions

Soap Homework

1. Read and color the attached handout about Lipids (Plate 17) from Griffin (1986).
2. Go to the following website and refresh yourself on what happens when thing dissolve:

   http://www.chem.iastate.edu/group/Greenbowe/sections/projectfolder/flashfiles/thermochem/solutionSalt.html

The link is also at summitchemistry.blogspot.com if you don't feel like typing the long web address in.

Capillary Action Homework

1. Read and color the attached handout about carbohydrates (Plate 15) from Griffin (1986).
2. Determine which bonds are polar and nonpolar in the ring form of glucose.
3. Look at cellulose (from the handouts in class, #16: Carbohydrates III). What types of intermolecular forces will cellulose exhibit?

Figure 5.3 *continued*

Fats Homework

1. Read and color the attached handout about Lipids (Plate 17) from Griffin (1986).
2. The unsaturated fatty acid shown on the handout is called a *cis* fatty acid because of how the carbons are arranged by the double bond:

There are also fatty acids that are called *trans* fatty acids, where the double bond looks like this:

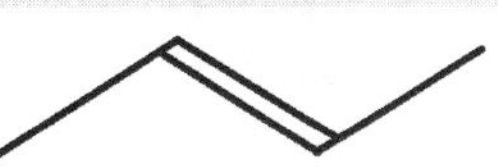

Question: How is the shape of a *trans* fatty acid going to be different from a *cis* fatty acid?

Cell Membrane Homework

1 Read and color the attached handout about Membrane Properties (Plate 33) from Griffin (1986).
2. The cell membrane is made up of billions of these particles:

Determine which sections of the molecule are polar and which sections are nonpolar.

Proteins Homework

1. Read and color the attached handouts about proteins and amino acids from Plates 18 and 19, Griffin (1986).

A quick note:

In the first handout, it shows two amino acids bonded together with a peptide bond. This would be a dipeptide.

Proteins are *polypeptides*—most proteins are made up of hundreds or thousands of amino acids.

Figure 5.3 *continued*

Boiling Point Homework

Determine the molar mass of each substance. Determine which parts of each molecule are polar and nonpolar.

Ammonia	Water	Acetone
Methanol	Methyl ether	Acetic acid
Nitrogen trifluoride	Hexane	Dihydrogen sulfide
Methane	Chloromethane	Ethanol

Table 5.1. Rubrics

Advanced	*Proficient*	*Basic*	*Beginner*	*No Evidence*
Group Presentation				
Presentation clearly, correctly, and concisely: - Explains what the topic is - Provides any background information the class may not know - Reviews ideas that are important to understand the topic The answer to the main question clearly and concisely: - Correctly applies an understanding of intermolecular forces - Correctly relates the type of bonding present to the type of intermolecular force present - Logically (but not necessarily correctly) explains how the topic works	Presentation clearly and correctly: - Explains what the topic is - Provides any background information the class may not know - Reviews ideas that are important to understand the topic The answer to the main question clearly: - Correctly applies an understanding of intermolecular forces - Correctly relates the type of bonding present to the type of intermolecular force present - Logically (but not necessarily correctly) explains how the topic works	Presentation correctly: - Explains what the topic is - Provides any background information the class may not know - Reviews ideas that are important to understand the topic The answer to the main question: - Correctly applies an understanding of intermolecular forces - Correctly relates the type of bonding present to the type of intermolecular force present - Logically (but not necessarily correctly) explains how the topic works	Presentation correctly: - Explains what the topic is - Provides some background information the class may not know - Reviews some ideas that are important to understand the topic The answer to the main question: - Applies an understanding of intermolecular forces - Correctly relates the type of bonding present to the type of intermolecular force present - Explains how the topic works, but with some confusion or unclarity	Presentation is missing: - An explanation of the topic - Background information - Review - The answer to the main question
Group Presentation: Visual				
- Visual is clear and easy to interpret. - Visual enhances presentation without distraction.	- Visual is easy to see and/or read. - Visual supports presentation without distraction.	- Visual is informative but unclear. - Visual is somewhat helpful for presentation, but also somewhat unhelpful.	- Visual is related to topic. - Visual distracts from presentation or doesn't help presentation.	- No visual, or visual is very confusing.

Table 5.1 *continued*

Advanced	*Proficient*	*Basic*	*Beginner*	*No Evidence*
Group work				
- All group members participated equally in the task. - All group members understand the topic of the group work. - All group members had equally important roles in the presentation.	- All group members participated in the task almost equally. - All members know the basics of the task, but some have difficulty putting the basics together into one explanation. - All group members had important roles in the presentation, but possibly unequal roles.	- All group members participated a fair amount in the task, but there were clearly dominant group members. - All group members know the basics of the topic and have complete if confused explanations. - All group members had a role in the presentation.	- All group members participated in the task at least a little. - Some group members can explain the task. - More than half the group had roles in the presentation.	- At least one person did not participate at all. - At least one group member is significantly confused. - Only 1 or 2 people had roles in the presentation.
Individual Portion				
- Clearly and concisely answers the question - Provides clear, concise, and accurate evidence to support answer - Evidence is based on an understanding of the intermolecular forces at work in the situation described - Clearly and concisely shows how evidence supports answer	- Clearly answers the question - Provides clear and accurate evidence to support answer - Evidence is based on an understanding of the intermolecular forces at work in the situation described - Clearly shows how evidence supports answer	- Answers the question - Provides accurate evidence to support answer - Evidence is based on an understanding of the intermolecular forces at work in the situation described - Shows how evidence supports answer	- Answers the question - Provides some evidence to support answer - Evidence relates to intermolecular forces, but not clearly - Shows how some evidence supports answer	- Does not answer the question - Does not provide evidence - Evidence is unrelated to intermolecular forces - Does not show how evidence supports answer

CHAPTER 6

Structuring Support for Students and Teachers

Maika Watanabe

This chapter is divided into two parts: structuring support for students, and structuring support for teachers. Part I discusses what educators at the featured schools do to help students who are struggling with the subject matter, as well as the rationale for these support structures. Part II discusses teacher professional development at all three featured schools.

Part I. Structuring Support for Students

All three high schools have implemented some innovative institutional mechanisms to help students who are struggling with the subject matter.

Destigmatizing Seeking Help, with Multiple Opportunities to Seek Tutoring. The film features how teachers destigmatize seeking help within the classroom; this section of the book discusses how educators have destigmatized seeking help outside of students' math or science classes.

For the first two weeks of every school year, all students at Summit Prep High School participate in hour-long lessons where they learn and practice schoolwide norms. Older peers help teach incoming students in mixed grade-level groups. Todd Dickson, a teacher at the school, noted in an interview that the sessions are "all designed to pass along the community feeling that everybody is here to help everybody succeed." "Leave no Husky [school mascot] behind," "If someone asks you for help, you have a duty to give your help," and "You are each other's best resources" are some of the norms that I observed posted in classrooms throughout the school. Dickson further explained, students "get a common message in every classroom, every year as they go through, that . . . it's your responsibility to ask if you're confused and it's your responsibility to help if someone asks." Asking for help is thus not seen as a weakness, or a sign of not being smart. Instead, seeking help shows that the student is taking responsibility for his/her own learning. A student I interviewed made clear that students understood and practiced these norms; he noted, "At other schools, if [students] ask other kids for help they'll say yes or no, but here, every time you ask people for help they will help you with what they can." Finally, the saying, "Mistakes are expected, inspected and respected" (which a Summit Prep teacher brought back from John Mahoney, a teacher in Washington, DC), encouraged what faculty members called "mathematical risk taking," wherein students would share ideas or try out new strategies with their group members, even when unsure of their accuracy.

At San Lorenzo High School, math teachers often repeated the saying, "Surface knowledge, confusion, deeper understanding." By identifying these stages of learning, faculty members teach students that confusion is part of the learning process, and is nothing to be ashamed about. In addition, the word "YET" was prominently displayed in many San Lorenzo math classrooms. I observed one math teacher pointing to the word YET in response to a student saying, "I don't get this." The student smiled and repeated, "I don't get this *yet*." The teacher praised the student for identifying that he needed help, and other students in his group set out to explain. On another day, I observed the following interaction as a teacher worked with a small group:

Teacher: What do these lines mean?
Student A: They crossed them out because they don't know what they're doing.
Student B: Excuse me?
Student A: YET (smile)

Students clearly adopted these norms as they regularly used the phrases in interactions with each other. There is such a difference in hope between the simple sentence, "I don't get this" and "I don't get this yet." Whereas "I don't get this" has a defeatist tone, "I don't get this yet" provides an opening for a teacher or peer to provide assistance. YET also communicates high expectations that with persistence and help, students will overcome the challenge.

Coupled with these schoolwide norms are multiple opportunities for students to ask for help from their teachers and peers. For example, all teachers at Summit Prep hold office hours (afterschool academic support) twice a week. Faculty members in a grade level split their office hours between the two days so students can spend at least an hour for each of their four subjects during the week. Teachers at High Tech High Bayshore similarly created an afterschool schedule so that students could get help from their English/History teacher two days a week and meet with their Math/Science teacher another two days during the week. At San Lorenzo High School, Laura Evans, a teacher, explained that there was an "expectation that [teachers'] doors were open for kids and we would be aggressive about pushing kids to see us at lunch." If students did not do their homework, many math teachers expected that they would come in during lunch or after school to complete their work.

While some dedicated professionals at traditional comprehensive high schools also offer office hours, Summit Prep has institutionalized this support structure across the board to encompass all teachers. It is important to note that Summit Prep was a new school, and its administrators were therefore able to hire like-minded educators who signed on to this set of responsibilities from the beginning. Even though High Tech High Bayshore administrators did not mandate that teachers stay after school for student tutoring, a high percentage of teachers stayed on to provide help to students. The same held true for the dedicated faculty in the math department at San Lorenzo High School, a large comprehensive high school.

Summit Prep also has a mandatory afterschool study hall (MASH) twice a week for students who have had difficulty turning in their homework. During MASH, students "have time set aside just to clear space to be able to get work done," noted Jon Deane, a teacher I interviewed. Similar to MASH, San Lorenzo High School created a "Homework Club" afters chool for students to complete their homework in all subject areas. One of the math teachers in the department earned release time from teaching to coordinate the afterschool club. Math teachers, as well as teachers from other subject areas, would rotate to offer help to students.

In addition to lunch hour and afterschool tutoring opportunities, all students at Summit Prep High School have an "independent learning" (IL) period, an hour-long study hall in which students can get help from peers or the proctoring teacher and/or work independently on homework assignments. Deane noted that IL was helpful for students because they could get started on their assignments and consult others if they got stuck before they headed home. The IL class helps to eliminate the stigma of seeking additional help from teachers and/or peers by virtue of the fact that every student is enrolled in IL and it is not considered a "remedial" class or an elective that students take in lieu of a foreign language/art/music. One of the students I interviewed at Summit Prep mentioned another reason IL appeared to work so well compared to traditional study halls: "I think detracking is really helpful, especially how like my whole class is in the same classes, so it's easier to get help." Students at Summit Prep can turn to each other for help during IL since they all share the same classes.

Simply offering office hours or instituting an IL class without addressing the stigma of "not understanding" will do little to make it comfortable for low-status, vulnerable students to seek help. Teachers must both praise students for taking the initiative to seek help and normalize confusion as part of the learning process.

Support classes provide additional space for students who are struggling academically to get help. At High Tech High schools, all students enroll in an X block, when students take electives or get tutoring. At the San Diego–based High Tech High International, students who have earned a grade of C or below enroll in tutoring during this time slot with a teacher from their grade level in the subject where they are struggling. Students with special needs enroll in tutoring with a resource specialist. This class may be as small as one or two students or as large as five or six students. Summit Prep instituted a math support class the year after I filmed classrooms. Dedicated math professionals (former teachers) pull students from IL classes two or three times a week to provide additional math help. These math teachers are involved in planning professional development activities for the math department at Summit, and are well versed in complex instruction; as a result, they are very knowledgeable about the math curricula at Summit and share the goals and teaching strategies of the Summit teachers. Students at San Lorenzo High School who were struggling in Algebra A, and who were viewed as likely to need help in Algebra B because of the larger class size and the faster pace, could opt into an Algebra B support class that they would take concurrently with the Algebra B class. Instruction in the support class, which met every other day, was tied directly to the content in the academic class. Teachers spoke one-on-one with students they were recommending to the support class in order to destigmatize the support class, emphasizing that the class was, according to Evans, a place to "continue the growth they had already shown." Another teacher described how teachers might say, "You know, you got a D in Algebra A, but there's something about you that gives us reason to be confident. Being in Algebra B support is a sign of our faith in you, not a sign that something is wrong with you."

Some readers might ask if support classes are a form of tracking, the sorting and grouping of students by perceived ability and the educational experiences that result. What differentiates the support class from more traditional tracking, where students are initially enrolled into remedial math, regular math, or honors math based on test scores, prior placement, teacher/counselor/parent recommendation, is that all students still engage in the same, college-bound, rigorous mathematics content in the academic math class. The support class bolsters students' skills so that they can achieve in the academic class. Membership in the support class does not preclude an advanced course of study in math and/or science, as membership in a remedial track would. In addition, at Summit Prep High School, students did not have to enroll in the support class the entire semester. They could move out of the support class if they and teachers deemed the extra support no longer necessary.

To be frank, creating support classes does indeed create an increase in the potential for status hierarchies to develop in small groups in the cohort's math class. Students likely know who is enrolled in the support class, and so teachers have a more difficult job ahead of them to address status hierarchies in the cohort math class. Because of schoolwide norms of praising students for seeking help and of appreciating the multiple, varied strengths of students in the featured classrooms at San Lorenzo High School and Summit Prep High School, students taking support classes at these schools did not express any shame in being simultaneously enrolled in the support class during interviews. The five Summit students I interviewed in 2010 all stated that they liked the support class because of the help they got in a small class[1] setting, with only five to eight students. One student specifically addressed whether there was a stigma associated with being in the class:

> At Summit, it's not like at other high schools. Other ones you know, they make fun of you and everything, and here it's like, "oh, all right." They're okay [with it] and some even want to join it because they need help on their homework. So I'm not ashamed of it.

Nonetheless, it is crucial to reiterate that schools cannot simply offer a support class without also implementing schoolwide norms that remove the stigma of seeking.

Allowing Courses to Be Retaken Without Offsetting the Sequence of Courses. Students at Summit Prep who, despite interventions[2] during the semester, have not demonstrated mastery of academic content or completed required work at the end of the school year, enroll in the Mandatory Academic Revision Sessions (MARS) during the winter or summer intersession. During the 8-week intersessions, all students at Summit take electives during the day. After the electives, students who participate in MARS meet from 3:15 to 5:15 on select days by subject area, as the calendar in Table 6.1 demonstrates. Students meet by grade level each day. Each subject has three sessions, with the exception of math, which has four meetings. Discretionary MARS sessions refer to sessions for students who need additional support.

Table 6.1. Mandatory Academic Revision Session (MARS) Calendar—January 2008

Monday	Tuesday	Wednesday	Thursday	Friday
7 Spanish 3:15–5:15PM	8 English 3:15–5:15 PM	9 Math 3:15–5:15 PM	10 Science 3:15–5:15 PM	11 History 3:15–5:15 PM
14 English 3:15–5:15 PM	15 Science 3:15–5:15 PM	16 Math 3:15–5:15 PM	17 Spanish 3:15–5:15 PM	18 English 3:15–5:15 PM
21 NO SCHOOL HOLIDAY	22 History 3:15–5:15 PM	23 Math 3:15–5:15 PM	24 English 3:15–5:15 PM	25 Science 3:15–5:15 PM
28 History 3:15–5:15 PM	29 Spanish 3:15–5:15 PM	30 Math 3:15–5:15 PM	31 Discretionary MARS	1 Discretionary MARS

Teachers help identify how many MARS sessions students need to attend. For example, a student who may have missed a quiz or test due to an absence and did not make it up during the school year may come in to take the assessment during one MARS session and not return for subsequent MARS sessions. Another student who did not meet the standard for a project may come in to a MARS session just to redo the project. Other students, who may have an overall semester grade that is below the passing mark, or who earned below a passing grade on the final exam, may attend all four MARS sessions in math and also come in for the Discretionary MARS classes.

Jon Deane described what he does during his MARS sessions:

> I've tried a bunch of different approaches. In the corner there may be two or three kids who just need to work on some assignments. And on another side there will be some students who really struggled with exponents and logs, and maybe we'll have them working together. Maybe the rest of the group is working on probability. So we might have different things going on [in the same MARS session].

During one MARS session that I observed, each small group of students received five problems to work on from a homework review sheet. While students worked on solving the problems, Deane circulated amongst the tables and conducted group quizzes once all group members felt they had worked out an answer (see DVD for more information on group quizzes).

A representative from each group then presented the process for finding the solution to one of the problems to everyone in the class. Afterwards, small groups worked on a poster describing one of the function families that they would later present to the entire MARS class. Deane made clear that this work would be important since students would be studying functions in more depth in pre-calculus.

One of the reasons that participation in MARS has less of a stigma compared to traditional summer school or remedial classes is that such a high percentage of students participate in at least one session of MARS. Deane noted that between first and second semester, 30 to 40 of his 100 math students participated in at least one MARS session, including students who needed to make up a test or project. At the end of the school year, he had about 22 students participating in at least one MARS session. The school's Director of Data Management estimated that on average, each teacher identified 15–20 students who needed extra support in a MARS class—not merely making up a test or project—during the 2009–2010 academic year.

At traditional comprehensive high schools, students who fail a course attend summer school or repeat the course during the next academic year. Deane explained that MARS was a better alternative, for three reasons: 1) Personal relationships between teachers and students were a hallmark of the school and MARS provided another opportunity for students to get more individualized help. 2) If teachers send students to a summer school at a different site, "you don't know what they've learned and how that sequences with your curriculum." 3) All of these opportunities support the cohort model, in which all students take the same classes, with the entire grade-level cohort moving to the next set of courses the following school year. If students repeated the whole course the following school year, it would destroy the cohort model and the college-bound sequence of classes.

That said, approximately 4.5% of Summit students during the 2009–2010 academic year were asked to take an additional class off-site to get additional help because they did not demonstrate proficiency during MARS. An additional 1.9% of Summit students have had to repeat the grade level due to special circumstances such as pregnancy, extended absences, or because they did not have the skills to advance to the next grade level across multiple subjects. It was difficult to get comparison data for the school district's other high schools, since state cutbacks to education forced the district to limit summer school enrollment, restricting it to only the students most in need (e.g., "seniors who are just a few credits shy of earning a diploma") (Sequoia Union High School District, 2010). Nonetheless, figures for Summit appear lower than what might be expected at larger high schools. Younger students, who are still figuring out work habits, made up a higher percentage of the Summit students who needed to retake a course, whereas at the end of the 2008–2009 school year, there were no failing grades in the eleventh grade. Summit faculty and staff were able to "catch" and support the vast majority of students with in-house interventions.

Deane recounted a student he worked with in both the ninth and tenth grades:

> He was the typical student who came in on the first day saying he hated math, and was never good at math. He wanted to do the bare minimum to get by, and every day of the ninth grade I fought him to do the bare minimum. But bare minimum for us means you have to keep working and working until you pass. He always did his work begrudgingly. He didn't want to do it, didn't like it. But over the course of the first year, and the fall of the second year, he softened. He could see the purpose of it and that he could do it. Last spring another student said, "I don't know if I can do it. I don't know if I can go to college." That first student looked at him and said, "If you don't want to go to college, why are you here at Summit? Why are you doing all of this work? Everyone here is going to college." This semester, his junior year, he looked me in the eye and said, "I don't have any MARS for any of my classes." *He found what was in himself to do all the work we had been asking him to do. It's really great when a student breaks free from all those supports and does well.*

I can just imagine the sort of pride the student had in reporting this news to his teacher, the type of pride that Deane expressed in retelling this story. There is often a confidence gap, where students would rather not attempt to do the work than be seen as "dumb" or not capable of doing the work. When teachers like Deane do not give up, in a school where there are institutional support mechanisms in place, students like the one described above begin to view academic challenges with a different frame of mind. With each new challenge tackled, the student's confidence grows, thereby influencing the student's willingness to try when faced with another challenge.

Similarly, students who fail a math course,[3] such as Algebra A, at San Lorenzo High School have the opportunity to retake the class the following semester and still reach Calculus. Why? Whereas math classes are usually two-semester, year-long courses at most traditional high schools, math at San Lorenzo advances by semester due to block scheduling. Students starting with algebra their first year in high school can typically not take

Table 6.2. Math Course Progression at San Lorenzo vs. Traditional High School (HS)

Semester	*San Lorenzo*	*Traditional HS*
Year 1: Fall	Algebra A	Algebra
Year 1: Spring	Algebra B	Algebra
Year 2: Fall	Geometry	Geometry
Year 2: Spring	Algebra 2/Trig	Geometry
Year 3: Fall	Calculus A	Algebra 2
Year 3: Spring	Calculus B	Algebra 2
Year 4: Fall		Pre-Calculus
Year 4: Spring		Pre-Calculus

Calculus at traditional high schools, as Table 6.2 shows, because of the time it takes to go through the sequence of courses.

In contrast, at San Lorenzo, students can actually take two semesters "off" from math, or even repeat two math courses and still reach Calculus. Rather than speed through the entire sequence, the math department encouraged students to take a break after Geometry and then wait until the next year to do Algebra 2. The math department also decided to offer a Math Analysis course for interested students either before they embarked on Calculus or after they completed Calculus.

Through these multiple opportunities to seek help and improve, students at Summit Prep High School and San Lorenzo are made aware of their "capacity to revise," an essential component to students maintaining positive outlooks on their futures (Fine, 2003, p. 46); students can make mistakes but also learn from them and make amends. In contrast, when adults attribute mistakes to students' character and do not give them opportunities to make changes, it becomes more difficult to stop students from internalizing failures and descending into a downward spiral. Fine cites research findings that show that wealthy or middle-class White students are more likely to receive second chances compared to poor students of color. She notes that mistakes that the former group make are seen as "developmental opportunities to learn," while poor students, particularly poor students of color, are "held personally accountable" for their errors, with long-term implications for their career and educational trajectories (Fine, 2003, p. 46). Not only are schools such as Summit Prep and San Lorenzo offering multiple chances to improve, they also make students more comfortable seeking help from teachers and peers by establishing schoolwide norms around mutual responsibility for learning, and by normalizing confusion as part of the learning process.

Part II. Structuring Support for Teachers

Mentoring for New Teachers. When I asked Laura Evans about professional development at San Lorenzo High School, her first response was, "It starts with hiring, and even before that, with taking on student teachers." San Lorenzo High School math teachers work with neighboring university credential programs to select student teachers who share the department's commitment to math equity and are committed to teaching in the geographical area. In the past, the math department has hired many of these student teachers, who have become well versed in the department's strong professional culture. Like San Lorenzo, Summit Prep has also hired former student teachers. Many Summit Prep teachers graduated from the teacher preparation program at neighboring Stanford University, where they took a course on complex instruction. Because of their shared preparation, these teachers have a common language and approach to teaching that unify them.

Next, at San Lorenzo High School, all math teachers teach at least one class period of Algebra to ninth graders, since, as Evans noted, "that's our conversation piece. That's something we can all work on together." Traditional, tracked high schools, which reward experienced teachers with the choice to teach only advanced levels of mathematics, often relegate the lowest track classes to the least experienced teachers (Finley, 1984), who encounter a different set of challenges than their more experienced colleagues who teach to a selective population of students. Teachers at San Lorenzo believe that the work involved in teaching Algebra is crucial to instilling the norms of the math department in students who come from a wide range of math experiences. Teaching students how to work well in groups, to recognize each other's multiple "smarts," and to take intellectual risks are all processes that are developed over the course of the students' entire math trajectory; thus, a positive Algebra experience is the first step towards achieving the department's goal to reduce D/F grades. It is also a matter of equity to make sure that all students have access to experienced math teachers. One way in which experienced teachers mentor new teachers at the school is by arranging the teaching schedule so that a new teacher has a planning period that coincides with a more experienced teacher's Algebra class. New teachers can thus observe what the experienced teacher does in his/her classroom, and then teach the same lesson the following day.

The High Tech High network of nine schools immerses new teachers in the High Tech High culture with a "New Teacher Odyssey" before the school year begins in San Diego. Teachers learn about High Tech High's four design principles: 1) personalization (e.g., personal portfolios about an area of individual interest), 2) adult world connection (internships and project-based learning), 3) common intellectual mission (no tracking), and 4) teacher as designer (interdisciplinary teams). Hillary Swanson, a teacher at High Tech High Bayshore who then went on to teach at High Tech High International, described the Odyssey Experience:

> Brand new teachers . . . get immersed in project-based learning. [We talk about] what are transitional presentations of learning?[4] What does it mean to have a teacher-driven school? What does it mean to have student-centered instruction? And you start developing projects and working in teams.

Experienced teachers share examples of project-based learning to incoming faculty members as a way to model High Tech High instruction.

Building a Professional Community for Curricular Planning, Problem Solving, and Support. At Summit Prep High School, San Lorenzo High School, and High Tech High Bayshore, teachers cultivate a strong professional culture with many hours of face-to-face meetings, sharing curricula, troubleshooting, providing emotional support, and developing long-range visions for the school/department.

The San Lorenzo math department spends approximately five days, from 9 A.M. to 3 P.M., immersed in Algebra teaching before the school year begins. Evans described one component of Algebra Week:

> We bond doing math together. . . . When kids do math together, there are all sorts of emotions [and] status issues that come up. There's something really grounding about doing math with your peers that reminds us of those emotions, and reminds us about what we care about in math learning. So we do math together. We probably do a problem a day.

Teachers also talk about sequence—moving units earlier or later. They model teaching practices such as providing a multiple-abilities orientation. Evans also spoke of how the department would engage in discussion to identify a dilemma and a goal that a teacher cannot address alone. In past years, the department chose the essential question, "How do we show every student that s/he is smart at math?" Participation in "Algebra Week," as well as the work to plan the week, is purely voluntary. Eventually, the department found some private funding to provide small teacher stipends for this unpaid work, but the practices developed first.

Conversations about algebra teaching continue during weekly, 90-minute afterschool meetings throughout the school year. Conversations begin with a check-in. Evans described what each member reported to the group:

> We would do a check-in. "This is where I am mathematically. This is what I'm really happy about and this is where I am struggling." I think there was something unique about how veteran teachers would talk about our struggle very publicly and that created a culture of "We're all struggling. We're going to struggle our entire lives. That's what learning to teach is." It's constant growth, and I think it made it safe for everyone to talk about what they struggled with. And if someone came to a meeting and broke down in tears around their struggle, we dropped whatever was on our plate and we helped them brainstorm through that. So we'd do a check-in and then we'd get to something we wanted to work on. Often we didn't have nearly enough time to talk about the thing we wanted to work on, and I remember feeling frustrated. "Oh, we did such a long check-in and we never got to really talk about X," but in hindsight, the growth that we got just from checking in with each other was huge in the way that it built our culture.

There is a strong sense that the department is a team, and that teachers are engaged in a collective struggle to improve the quality of math teaching and learning for students. Drawing on my own experience as a teacher, I indicated surprise that the vast majority of math teachers participated in these voluntary meetings for so long after school. Evan's response:

> When we hire, I don't know if we ever explicitly say, "You are expected to come." I think it's more like "And you get to have an hour and a half every week to talk about [how things are going]." You know this is going on prior to getting hired. When I walked in, all I could think of was, "Thank God. I need this."

Sometimes, because of the check-ins, teachers offer to observe other teachers' algebra classes. Other subject-area teachers, like those who teach geometry, meet once every two weeks afterschool based on the assumption that the practices all teachers are using in Algebra are translating into smoother Geometry classes, as students become accustomed to math department norms. In addition to these subject-area team meetings, department meetings take place once every two months to take care of school-related business. These department meetings are more typical of traditional high school department meetings where day-to-day curricula are not necessarily the central focus.

Teachers at San Lorenzo also volunteer to coordinate curricula by subject for all teachers who teach the class. These teachers may map out a timeline of curricular ideas for the department-developed units and distribute revised student handouts based on conversations during Algebra Week or the 90-minute afterschool meetings.

Teachers at High Tech High Bayshore also met frequently, compared to teachers at traditional, large public high schools with monthly faculty meetings. Grade-level team teachers (science/math teacher and English/history teacher) met at least once a week, if not daily, to discuss common students and curricula. In addition, faculty members met twice a week for hour-long meetings as a whole school to participate in study groups, ongoing professional development, and project tuning protocols.

Whole-school faculty meetings took different shapes based on faculty-identified needs. Swanson described how study groups

> looked at how to support English Language Learner students, or how to support low socioeconomic status or free/reduced lunch students. Or how to make advisories work better.

Maja Catipovic, another teacher at High Tech High Bayshore, also mentioned that teachers participated in several conversations with a High Tech High specialist on developing student writing. Teachers could also volunteer to organize a session, if they were so inclined. For example, Swanson mentioned that she led a session on classroom management techniques from a book she read. The Coalition of Essential Schools developed the project-tuning protocol as a way to allow teachers to reflect and offer feedback on a work-in-progress. Swanson described how the protocols worked at High Tech High Bayshore, with a teacher bringing some student work to share:

> We'd break into smaller groups or maybe we'd do it as an entire group sometimes. Teachers would say, "What were the instructions you gave to the student? What are the rubrics that you graded them with? Did you think about asking [students] this?" So the teacher got feedback and she would tune her project. . . .

Through these protocols, teachers shared curricula across disciplines, worked on rubrics, and discussed how to structure projects.

Seminars and Conferences. Teachers across all three sites also engaged in intensive, teacher-directed seminars and conferences for professional development. Teachers at Summit Prep receive 40 days of site-based teacher professional development in one school year. Teachers meet before school starts in August; in addition, they participate in intensive, daily, month-long inquiries during the intersessions in January and at the end of the school year while students take their elective classes. Summit Prep faculty members do not teach electives; instead, Summit Prep brings in professional artists and musicians, affiliated with two organizations, to teach elective classes.

Teachers identify topics for professional development. Past topics have included designing complex instruction lessons, working with English language learners, and modifying instruction for students with special needs. Summit Prep faculty members often research and develop the training and facilitate discussions themselves, as administrators recognize their curiosity and talent. Sometimes Summit Prep invites outside speakers. For example, Summit Prep faculty members had university professors present different research methods and provide information on special education laws.

Like the teachers at Summit Prep and San Lorenzo High School, teachers at High Tech High Bayshore participated in intensive, week-long professional development prior to the start of each school year. All teachers in the High Tech High network fly to San Diego for a day or two to participate in the High Tech High Symposium, where teachers brainstorm curricular projects across sites. Each High Tech High would then have its own 3-day retreat to gear up for the new school year. Week-long workshops, called Institutes, also convene in the fall, spring, and summer, where High Tech High network teachers fly to a site in San Diego and observe another High Tech High in operation during the school year. Participants take a workshop with a practicing teacher, observe a project in action, and speak to students about what they are doing.

Math faculty at San Lorenzo also attend and present together at professional conferences, such as at the California Mathematics Council conferences in Asilomar, CA. In past years, before the state budget crisis, the district would provide partial funds for teachers to attend professional conferences. Math teachers at San Lorenzo who attended Asilomar would then report on the experience to the department members who gathered at one teacher's home.

Developing a Unified Vision. One theme that stood out to me as I visited the three featured high schools was the strong, shared vision of teaching that teachers actively work towards. Teachers at High Tech High are committed to project-based learning and no tracking. San Lorenzo High School math teachers are engaged in the challenge of making all students realize their math "smarts." Since the summer of 2010, Summit Prep High

School math teachers have been engaged in intensive discussion about how to create "powerful math learners." There is a collective commitment to achieving these missions. In all of the many professional development meetings that teachers attend, these ideas are wrestled with, implemented, reflected upon, and brought back to the table.

There is a lesson here for those who are building a new school: Hiring like-minded colleagues will greatly facilitate progress towards achieving your vision. This is the story of Summit Prep and High Tech High. It starts with developing a well-articulated mission for the school. Before you can begin to think about the logistics of school location and hiring, the mission must be carefully considered.

If I were at a school without this shared vision, I would start small, having deep conversations with a few teachers, to identify, as Evans describes, "a dilemma that can't be solved alone, a goal for the department or school." A few teacher leaders can build a movement, as happened at San Lorenzo High School. The strong professional culture in the math department at San Lorenzo High School developed slowly over fifteen years. Evans explained that one of the impetuses behind department change was a negative Western Association of Schools and Colleges (WASC) report. When students were asked, "How do you feel in your math classrooms?" responses were negative; Evans explained that "students who were interviewed just felt like they were isolated [in their classrooms] and that math was something they couldn't do." A few teachers decided they wanted to make some changes. One change was to move from a 50-minute period to a block schedule. Another change was for teachers *and* students to collaborate around mathematics. Evans explained some of the thinking behind these changes:

> We teachers are teaching in isolation. Of course our students are going to feel this way. So several teachers started getting together and talking about "how do we make this more accessible?" and one of the ideas was, "well, if we're collaborating, why don't we have students collaborate around mathematics?" So it sort of morphed slowly into collaborating around curriculum, around supporting kids around how to do groupwork, meeting regularly and talking about what is going well, what's not going well and why, and then of course asking students the same things around mathematics. But I think we really put the focus on "we're all learning here as a math department, even those of us who have been doing groupwork a long time. That's what makes this job still interesting." So we regularly try to collaborate not just around our curriculum but also how to teach, how to make complex instruction work, and how to support our kids overall.

The strong department culture results in a common discourse across classes, helping students build on practices from semester to semester. Inquiry groups can be powerful spaces for teachers to engage in discussion that is not ordinarily scheduled into the workday (Watanabe, 2007).

Take-away Points

- "Support for students" must be coupled with creating a schoolwide culture that makes it okay to ask for help. Merely offering tutoring without creating schoolwide norms around confusion as a natural stage of learning do not make it feel safe for low-status students to seek help. Multiple opportunities for revision help empower students.
- As Evans said in the DVD, you need a teacher community you can talk to about the complexity of detracking.
- I am struck by how much face-to-face time teachers at these schools have regarding curricula and by the positive energy surrounding these meetings. I am reminded of my own experience as a teacher where we had monthly faculty meetings, with many overworked teachers multitasking and grading papers in the back of the room. Even with once-a-week grade-level team meetings that I participated in, most of the conversations were about struggling students and less about curricula. The shared commitment to collective growth through in-depth examinations of curricula and pedagogy at the three featured schools is noteworthy.

Notes to Chapter 6

1. Summit faculty and administrators refer only 3%–4% of the total population of students to the math support class through a student support team (SST) process or through math teacher recommendation; Individualized Education Plans (IEPs) place an additional 3%–4% of the total population in the support class.

2. For example, *grade-level teams* meet weekly for an hour to identify students who are having difficulties (e.g., reading comprehension, taking notes), and to develop a plan to help the student gain needed skills in one class or across classes. Similarly, at High Tech High Bayshore and San Lorenzo High School, teachers, parents, administrators, and students would meet for a Student Support Team (SST) meeting to create a plan to address academic difficulties.

3. When students failed a class, teachers would have one-on-one conversations with students about why they needed to repeat the class. Usually, attendance, homework, or off-task behavior in class were the main factors. Evans said that most students could identify the factors themselves, and teachers framed the conversations positively. For example, teachers would describe how it took a

few months until the student "decided to be a learner." While students showed tremendous improvement towards the end of the semester, this progress was not enough to offset the lack of work at the beginning.

4. A Transitional Presentation of Learning is a required student presentation at the end of each academic year to reflect on the student's progress in front of a panel of teachers, students, community members, and/or industry experts.

References

Fine, M. (2003). *The psychological and academic effects on children and adolescents of structural facilities' problems, exposure to high levels of under-credentialed teachers, substantial teacher turnover, and inadequate books and materials.* Retrieved August 31, 2010, from www.decentschools.org/experts.php?sub-per

Finley, M. K. (1984). Teachers and tracking in a comprehensive high school. *Sociology of Education, 57,* 233–243.

Sequoia Union High School District. (2010). *2010 Summer School.* Retrieved October 21, 2010, from http://www.sequoiadistrict.org/2044101221840523/site/default.asp

Watanabe, M. (2007). Lessons from a teacher inquiry group about tracking: Perceived student choice in course-taking and its implications for detracking reform. *Teachers College Record, 109*(9), 2136–2170.

CHAPTER 7

Frequently Asked Questions

Maika Watanabe

This chapter addresses frequently asked questions in a "Q&A" format. I put together this list of questions after showing this film to K–12 teachers, school administrators, university professors, researchers, professional development staff, and journalists at the annual meeting of the American Educational Researchers Association as well as to in-service and pre-service teachers in university-level classes at UC Berkeley and San Francisco State University.

1. How do teachers prepare for state standardized tests using this approach? Were the classroom scenes filmed after the test?

Classroom scenes were not filmed after the test. Teachers use this teaching approach throughout the school year. Teachers incorporated test preparation without sacrificing the logic and beauty of their curricula.

San Lorenzo teachers "helped students bridge from the language of instruction to the language of assessment," as described by Carlos Cabana, a math teacher. Language used in problems on the state standardized tests can be particularly difficult to understand, as the following two released questions from the California Standards Test (CST) demonstrate:

1. Is the equation $3(2x - 4) = -18$ equivalent to $6x-12 = -18$?

   A Yes, the equations are equivalent by the Associative Property of Multiplication.

   B Yes, the equations are equivalent by the Commutative Property of Multiplication.

   C Yes, the equations are equivalent by the Distributive Property of Multiplication over Addition.

   D No, the equations are not equivalent.

(California Department of Education, 2010a, p. 6).

19. The chart below shows an expression evaluated for four different values of x.

x	$x^2 + x + 5$
1	7
2	11
6	47
7	61

Josiah concluded that for all positive values of x, $x^2 + x + 5$ produces a prime number.

Which value of x serves as a counterexample to prove Josiah's conclusion false?

A 5
B 11
C 16
D 21

(California Department of Education, 2010a, p. 9)

Language on these sample questions, such as "associative," "counterexample," "prime number," tests for vocabulary comprehension. San Lorenzo teachers worked on making students familiar with the language so that, as Cabana explained, the language

> wouldn't get in students' way . . . because [the student population of] San Lorenzo is 70–75% . . . students for whom academic English doesn't match their home language, either because they're non-native English speakers, or because they're working-class students [who] don't necessarily hear academic English outside the classroom.

Unless teachers specifically teach the language of assessment, students may know the mathematics but be unable to answer the questions.

Secondly, teachers, such as Cabana, worked to ensure "that the test prep curriculum spirals in the same way that our curriculum spirals and that meant developing explicit materials." Laura Evans described some of these materials:

> We as a department have come up with what we call 50 sheets—50 small nuggets of things that you can throw in around homework, around classwork, around a warm-up, something quick we can use to address those little bits. The way we are characterizing our curriculum is we still have what we want to keep deep. The standards that truly are needed for kids to continue to learn more mathematics, we still are trying to do those deeply. And then the other things that it's impossible to do deeply because of time constraints, we are willing to throw in on a more shallow basis.

Finally, San Lorenzo teachers also taught students how to take multiple-choice tests. Cabana noted that many of their students thought "you should be able to do a multiple-choice test in your head. And they don't realize that you have to show your work to avoid common mistakes." Teachers taught students about distracting answers that test writers include on multiple-choice tests that are part of the process to find the solution, but are not the answer to the question.

Math teachers at Summit Prep High School are starting "CST Thursdays" in the fall of 2010, where students will focus on preparing for the standardized tests, as an alternative to completely changing the nature of the curricula throughout the academic year. At High Tech High Bayshore, most teachers did some standardized test preparation for students by way of practicing a few problems from sample tests in the weeks before the test, and/or doing a problem a day during the warm-up at the start of the class period; however, teachers did this on their own without direct pressure from the school. It helps that at charter schools like Summit Prep High School and High Tech High, the teachers had the support of like-minded administrators who did not put undue emphasis on standardized test score performance compared to other measures of school success, such as the percentage of students who fulfilled 4-year college admission requirements. At San Lorenzo High School, faculty members in the math department spent a lot of time defending their teaching practices to the district through the use of data.

2. How did administrators get AP and honors labels affixed to their detracked classes?

While a school may designate a course as honors for local purposes, the University of California (UC) awards special honors credit to eleventh and twelfth-grade classes that meet special requirements. Administrators and teachers at a school submit course information to earn the UC honors label designation. Teachers turn in course objectives, a course outline, student assignments, texts and/or instructional materials, and information on instructional and assessment methods (as well as a list of laboratory work for lab science courses) to the university committee. Based on the submitted justification and documentation, the university committee determines whether the coursework is comparable to collegiate level courses. The University of California automatically accepts AP courses that have gone through the College Board AP Audit Process.

3. What is the attrition rate at the charter schools? Do you just weed out students who can't perform well in the classes, allowing for a more homogeneous makeup of students in advanced classes?

Part of the difficulty in answering this question is that public data about student retention are difficult to locate. In California, the state legislature passed a law to provide all students with a single lifetime school identifier number in 2002; however, the state has not funded the measure, impeding its implementation (Harvard Civil Rights Project, 2005). Table 7.1 displays California Department of Education (2010b) data for the number of exit records by exit codes during the 2007–2008 school year for Summit Prep, a public high school near Summit, as well as the school district. I chose the top five exit codes for each setting, with the exception of "Graduated, HS diploma" to create this table. The percentage of students leaving Summit Prep to enroll in another public school is much lower than that of another area high school as well as of the district as a whole, thereby providing evidence that Summit Prep does not simply push out large percentages of students.

According to Todd Dickson, who is currently the Executive Director of Summit Prep Charter High School, the school has an 82% retention rate (the percentage of students who begin Summit as ninth graders and graduate as seniors). This retention rate is high, compared to district high schools and other charter schools that release this information. For example, San Francisco Bay Area KIPP Schools had an average of 54% retention across five schools, for the 2004 entering cohort (Woodworth, David, Guha, Wang, & Lopez-Torkos, 2008, p. 14). Dickson characterized most of the attrition at Summit as due to students moving out of the area, or moving to larger high schools. Summit has only a 1% dropout rate (only 1% did not graduate with a high school diploma), and a 1.5% expulsion

Table 7.1 Exit Records by Exit Codes During the 2007–08 School Year

	# of students divided by total number of students		
Exit Code	*Summit Prep Charter High*	*Public High School in district, a few miles from Summit*	*District*
Enroll another pub CA school	5%	11.2%	12.2%
Enroll in private CA school	0.2%	.05%	0.4%
Enroll outside CA	0.7%	.05%	0.7%
Enroll adult ed program	0.2%	2.1%	1.8%
Entered health care facility	0.2%	.01%	0.3%
Entered inst for HS diploma	n/a	2.6%	0.8%
Moved to another country	n/a	1%	0.8%
Exceptional needs w/certification	n/a	.07%	0.5%
Other (count as dropout)	n/a	0.05%	1%

Source: California Department of Education (2010b)

rate for bringing drugs, using alcohol, or being involved in a severe fight. According to Dickson, the expulsion figure is similar to the district average, and the dropout rate is below the district average.

Low initial enrollment and some student attrition at High Tech High Bayshore contributed, in part, to its closing after two years; however, based on interviews with teachers at High Tech High Bayshore, the students who left were more likely to be high-achieving students who could achieve in area high schools, than low-achieving students (see Epilogue for more info). Data similar to the table above were not available for HTH Bayshore. Based on interviews with teachers who taught at three High Tech High schools in San Diego, attrition is comparatively not a problem at the High Tech Highs in that city. The schools do occasionally lose a few students because they move, or they feel the model is not a good fit for them. For example, one teacher noted that the students who leave

> are more comfortable with a more traditional model. They miss football games, they prefer covering more topics in less depth, doing worksheets and taking tests. Some leave because they don't pass their [Transitional Presentations of Learning] or tire of having to repeat grades, and some are expelled for misbehavior . . . [but] my sense was these were few in number. Since we had so few students and teachers had close relationships with them, losing any students was a big deal.

Teachers reported high retention rates, and rejected claims that the school pushed out students who could not perform well academically.

4. Do you have behavior problems in your classroom?

Teachers answered "yes" to this question, often with smiles, but in 47 hours of filming, I did not observe any direct, ugly confrontations between teachers and students. While my presence or the presence of the camera might have had some effect, I believe these did little to change the class climate, since we were in the classrooms for such extended periods of time.

One of the central tenets of Dr. Elizabeth Cohen's work on complex instruction is that status is situational; it is not a personality trait. I am reminded of a high school student I observed in one student teacher's tracked science class, who would proclaim loudly, "I hate this class," and behave poorly by not listening to the teacher and talking to his peers about unrelated material. Later that day I happened to observe this same student in a P. E. class, where he took a clear leadership role. The student excelled in soccer, and in an informal game, he carefully passed the soccer ball to a female student to score the winning goal, even though he clearly could have scored the goal himself. His strengths were being aware of his teammate's position, knowing how much it would mean to his teammate to score the goal, and adjusting his pass so she could reach the ball. At the end of the class period, he behaved respectfully towards his teacher, listening to her directions and shushing other students to do the same. This student was not a "behavior problem"; rather, he acted out in certain contexts.

Complex instruction asks why a student is not participating or is behaving poorly. In many situations, a student who is misbehaving has low status and would rather act out rather than "look dumb." I often tell my credential students to consider the student whose behavior they are finding problematic as their absolute favorite. It is up to the teacher to figure out why that student is his/her favorite. Changing perspective in this way helps teachers think about the intellectual strengths of the student. Locating and publicly praising these intellectual strengths raises the student's status and helps the student feel "wanted" in class. As Claude Steele stated in a presentation he gave to Stanford Teacher Education Program students in the Winter quarter of 2007, you can't function well if you feel like you don't belong. Once students feel safety and belonging, they can focus in on the task and remember the content; otherwise, they are distracted and do not perform as well in research experiments he conducted.

Some of our featured teachers were masterful classroom managers who excelled at communicating clear expectations and making students feel valued. For example, Laura Evans is featured in the film doing a participation quiz, which helps to build positive group and classwide norms (see Group Norms section of DVD). She praises one group for engaging with the problems "all the way through." She tells another group that the group "started out rough" with one male student "running the show." She then praises this same group when a female student "stepped up" and figured out something the male student couldn't figure out. The group "recovered well" because other people began "touching the pieces and you guys were thinking together." When Evans publicly shares her evaluation of the participation quiz, she communicates her expectation that all students should be engaged with the problems during the entire class period. Students see that their participation or nonparticipation affects their assessment and ultimately, their learning. In addition, Evans uses status treatments to make students like the female student feel valued by the group and by the class. Of course, she sometimes has to wait to get everyone to quiet down so everyone in class can hear a classmate present at the overhead. But the tone in the classroom is very positive and respectful.

Before San Lorenzo High School fully detracked algebra by enrolling all incoming ninth graders into algebra, however, the same skilled teachers who were experiencing success with classroom management in the tracked algebra classes faced challenges with behavior in their low-tracked pre-algebra classes. Laura Evans describes the class:

> We found that many of the kids were very rebellious of the curriculum, even though they didn't necessarily have a strong foundation for fractions or in multiplying. They were resisting the curriculum because they knew they were being categorized as the kids who don't get it, the kids who aren't good at math. Another teacher and I decided, "Why don't we try teaching them algebra and see what happens?" So one day, I said [to the pre-algebra class], "H`ere are your choices. We can continue to do the curriculum we are doing or you guys can start learning algebra, and if you can succeed we can give you algebra credit and you can move on." And they were very excited about it. They took it on, they took it on well, and most of them moved on to the second part of the algebra [Algebra B] as opposed to having to start from the beginning [Algebra A]. So emotionally, they bought into it, that "I'm learning something rigorous. This is my new chance now that I'm starting high school." So there wasn't this sense of "I'm a failure and I continue to be a failure." It's "I'm starting new."

In this case, teachers were able to minimize negative behavior in classrooms by challenging students with more rigorous curricula and getting rid of the lower-track designation. By changing the context, "behavior problems" lessened considerably.

5. My students are not like your students.You must have students who are extremely motivated. Isn't self-selection a key factor in your success?

Unfortunately, Summit Prep does not have data to compare its students with the applicants to Summit Prep High School who did not get in, which would be the best way to control for self-selection. Summit Prep has analyzed data, however, to show that the school is not educating just the high-achieving students in the district. The incoming ninth graders are similar to their counterparts at other district high schools in terms of their California standardized test scores in language arts and math in middle school. In addition, teachers like Jon Deane (see Chapter 6) also recounted plenty of stories about students who did not complete work initially. Teachers had to implement many supports to convince these students that they could succeed academically.

Finally, the complex instruction approach would encourage teachers to find out why the student was exhibiting "unmotivated" behavior in class. The "unmotivated" behavior may stem from a status hierarchy in the small group or whole class, and the teacher may need to work to raise the status of the student publicly, so the other students value the student's contributions and the student adopts a more productive presence in the class.

6. What type of support do you provide English Language Learners in class?

Dr. Rachel Lotan, who was one of the founding developers of complex instruction with Dr. Elizabeth Cohen, emphasizes that addressing the development of academic language is an important component of building an equitable classroom. Oral and written proficiency in the language of instruction is an additional dimension of heterogeneous classrooms. In a course she teaches in the Stanford Teacher Education Program, Dr. Lotan often refers to bilingual and multilingual students as "national treasures." These references help set the tone for all students to see multilingualism as an intellectual asset.

In order to have non-ELL students appreciate the challenges of being an English Language Learner, Dr. Lotan leads her pre-service teacher credential candidates in an exercise called Master Designer from Cohen's (1994) *Designing Groupwork,* though with a twist. After a first round in English, a Master Designer has to explain a hidden design made with tangrams in a language other than English to the rest of the small group. The other members of the group have to create the same design based on the Master Designer's directions. They can ask questions in English, but the Master Designer is not allowed to use English to respond. Members of the group use each other as resources to replicate the design. This exercise has also been done with middle and high school students, to sensitize students to issues of language. After the exercise, students discussed what was challenging and what helped the group complete the design. For example, since the students were already familiar with the purpose and the process of the task, some groups began the second round with a mini-vocabulary lesson.

Dr. Lotan mentions that teachers should be explicit about the strategies a student might use to get access to the content. For example, teachers should present to all students key discipline-specific vocabulary or language-stems that will help the student talk/write about the material. For example, in science, "We hypothesize that . . ." "These data suggest that . . ." "We conclude that . . ." are phrases that scientists use to present their findings. English Language Learners should be told that they can use their native language with other speakers to help them comprehend material. In footage of the group quiz in the film, viewers will notice that when Laura Evans leaves the group, group members hurriedly converse in Spanish to go over the problem. In addition, in a *TESOL Journal* article titled "Beyond Sheltered Instruction," Bunch, Abram, Lotan, and Valdés (2001) recommend adding "synopses in the margins of readings to provide cues to the topic of each section of text" rather than summarizing the primary source, which would limit access to "authentic texts" (p. 31).

For a comprehensive examination of research and teaching practices to support the academic language development of students in complex instruction classrooms, I highly recommend the *TESOL Journal* article, mentioned above, as well as "Developing Language and Mastering Content in Heterogeneous Classrooms" by Rachel A. Lotan, published in the 2008 book, *The Teacher's Role in Implementing Cooperative Learning in the Classroom,* edited by Robyn Gillies, Adrian Ashman, and Jan Terwel.

High Tech High Bayshore hired a support coordinator for the high percentage of English Language Learners. While paraprofessionals in special education are common in traditional public high schools, an English language support coordinator is rare in California, especially in the climate of severe educational budget cuts. The English language support coordinator rotated among classrooms, simultaneously providing in-class support to students and taking note of classroom demands. She also contacted families of English Language Learners to develop plans to support these students.

7. Isn't this just about good teaching? Can't you just do complex instruction in tracked classes?

Complex instruction can be done in tracked classrooms, but the outcomes there are not as effective for several reasons. If students do not take the equivalent of three years of college prep mathematics or take at least two years of laboratory science before they graduate high school, they can not fulfill the requirements to apply to most four-year universities. So even if teachers used Complex instruction in a remedial math class or a lower tracked, non-laboratory science class, these students are already effectively restricted from access to four-year universities. Moreover, research has consistently demonstrated that students of color from low socioeconomic backgrounds are disproportionately assigned to the lower academic tracks, *irrespective* of their academic achievement (Lucas, 1999; Mickelson, 1999). This discrepancy stems from a complex interplay between institutional barriers (biased teachers and counselors, lack of communication about implications of course-taking) and students' conceptions of their likely fit with and success in higher-tracked courses (Yonezawa, Wells, & Serna, 2002). Thus, even when there are "quality" lower-tracked classes using complex instruction, students of color from low socioeconomic backgrounds are being excluded from access to college-bound courses. Conversely, detracking and using complex instruction in the classroom helps to reverse the persistence of race- and class-based inequality in American schools, providing more equal access to higher education for all students.

In addition, the hierarchy of classes at a tracked school makes it all but impossible not to label and treat groups of students with corresponding expectations. Students internalize and meet these teacher and peer expectations for their performance. They know that they are in a lower-tracked math or science course and adopt negative math/science learner identities. Complex instruction shakes up these images by recognizing the multiple intelligences required to think mathematically and scientifically, but this can only happen when the classes are truly heterogeneous. In tracked schools, the power of the class label overshadows students' seeing one another's multiple "smarts" in the math or science classroom; students think they are only "smart" for the lower-tracked class and their self-conceptions do not carry over into thinking of themselves in a more generalized context as capable math or science learners.

8. Not all of our subject matter can be presented through open-ended complex problems. Do you do complex problems every day?

It depends on the teacher and the school. At one end of the continuum, students at San Lorenzo High School worked in groups everyday on math problems during the blocked period. At Summit Prep High School, one physics teacher usually did one complex, groupworthy problem/lab per unit. At High Tech High Bayshore, there was always a project associated with each unit, but teachers would intersperse mini-lessons during the unit.

9. How do you grade students on the complex problem assignments that they complete in groups?

The founders of complex instruction caution teachers not to give group grades or to individually grade a student for group participation. Dr. Lotan explained the problems with these assessment techniques in an interview with me:

> When a teacher gives the group a group grade, it might create resentment because some kids might feel that they contributed more than others and so to get a grade that doesn't reflect their contribution is "unfair." Another issue around grading in groupwork that I find problematic is grading for participation. Very often, teachers think that saying "you will get five points or ten points given the amount of participation that you show" will motivate kids who don't participate to participate. However, when I show tapes of small groups where [low-status kids] don't participate—not because they don't want to, but because the group won't let them—people realize that "oh my gosh! We are blaming the victim." We are punishing the kid for the fact that others won't let that kid participate, or won't hear his/her participation. So I'm very wary of doing that and I usually recommend not to do it. But sometimes, people do it anyway. It is a thorny issue.

So what should teachers grade? Dr. Lotan responded first that we do not have to grade every assignment; feedback is much more important and useful. Teachers can give quality feedback about the group product without necessarily assigning a letter grade. Students' desire to perform well in front of peers could be the prime motivator for a strong product, as opposed to a letter grade.

In *Designing Groupwork,* Elizabeth Cohen recommends that teachers grade individual work that comes out of the group product. Dr. Lotan concurs. For example, a teacher might present a problem similar to one completed during groupwork on an individual test or an individual essay. To encourage students to pay attention to the quality of their discussion and product, students can be told about research that demonstrated that "the better the quality of the group discussion and product, the better will be the individual performance of group members" (Cohen, Lotan, Scarloss, Schultz, & Abram, 2002, p. 1050).

Readers will notice that the teachers featured in this DVD address grading differently. Jon Deane and Angela Knotts grade the individual write-up. Howard Shen and Maja Catipovic include rubrics for the group presentations as well as the individual write-ups. Laura Evans discusses in the film that she gives group quizzes and tests as well as individual tests (see Interdependence section), but she weighs more heavily the individual assessments when it comes to determining final grades.

As Dr. Lotan mentioned in the above quote, assessment is a very difficult issue, one I continue to struggle with as I assign group presentations in my teacher credential classes. A few conclusions on assessment: If teachers are to give group grades, they must be very attentive to the group dynamics to ensure that low-status students are not being excluded and everyone is actively engaging and contributing productively. In addition, evaluation criteria must be clearly spelled out and distributed to students before they begin working on a project. Finally, if you do give group grades, they should not be weighed as heavily as individual assessments when it comes to final grades.

10. If excessive absenteeism is a problem in a class, how does one manage the progress within the groups if certain roles are not being met?

At San Lorenzo, students worked on problems together as a group. If one member was absent, the team captain would take on an additional role. If only half of the group is present, the remaining team members split the vacant roles. To encourage on-time arrivals and regular class participation, some teachers such as Laura Evans have students fill out a chart at the beginning of class where students earn points for on-time arrivals

(2 points), tardy arrivals (1 point), and completed homework (10 points). When students see that their attendance, classwork, and homework translate not only into points but also into a better understanding of the content, it can help encourage students to be accountable to themselves and to their group by attending class. In addition, when students feel a sense of belonging in the class (see answer to question 4), they are more likely to show up everyday.

Absenteeism poses more of a problem when the group is creating a product that will take longer than one blocked period. Teachers have made adjustments to group deadlines, when needed, or have modified the assignment to take into consideration an absent group member.

11. How do you convince an academically high-status student that s/he doesn't "know it all" and will benefit from groupwork?

All students have an area they need to work on. The key is to identify a learning agenda for every student. One math teacher leader found that many high-status students still needed to work on multiple representations of the content or to work on being able to verbally justify answers. He has found that groupwork helps these high-status students strengthen these areas. One way to communicate that a student can learn from his/her group is to ask a group quiz question that is challenging to the high-status student, one that s/he will need to consult group members to answer.

12. I want to do complex instruction in my class. Where do you suggest I start?

Designing Groupwork: Strategies for a Heterogeneous Classroom, by Elizabeth G. Cohen, provides detailed information on complex instruction and includes an appendix with exercises to help students talk about groupwork norms. Workshops on complex instruction in the mathematics classroom are frequently offered by teachers (including Laura Evans, who is featured in this film) in the San Francisco Bay Area and in Seattle. Please contact me at watanabe@sfsu.edu for more current information on dates and locations of these workshops, as the network of teacher experts who offer workshops does not yet have an official home. Finally, as Laura Evans noted in the film itself, it is best to team up with other colleagues to offer each other support as you embark on this curricular reform. Working in teams with colleagues can help you get feedback as well as build a collective library of groupworthy tasks in less time than it would take if you worked alone. If every team member works on one or two groupworthy problems during the summer and is ready to share them at the beginning of the school year, you would find yourself with several problems to start the year.

Complex instruction is not easy to implement, but the rewards for students and teachers make the challenge worthwhile. It takes time to write groupworthy tasks, constant attention to group norms, and practice to assign competence to low-status students, but I have noticed that once the culture is established, the classes run very smoothly. Writing a groupworthy task for students is a groupworthy task in and of itself.

References

Bunch, G. C., Abram, P. L., Lotan, R. A., & Valdés, G. (2001). Beyond sheltered instruction: Rethinking conditions for academic language development. *TESOL Journal, 10*(2–3), 28–33.

California Department of Education. (2010a). *Released test questions: Algebra I.* Retrieved October 27, 2010, from http://www.cde.ca.gov/ta/tg/sr/documents/rtqalg1.pdf

California Department of Education. (2010b). *Dropouts: Number of exit records by exit code, 2007–2008.* Retrieved October 18, 2010, from http://dq.cde.ca.gov/dataquest/

Cohen, E. G. (1994). *Designing groupwork: Strategies for the heterogeneous classroom, second edition.* New York: Teachers College Press.

Cohen, E. G., Lotan, R., Scarloss, B., Schultz, S. E., & Abram, P. (2002). Can groups learn? *Teachers College Record, 104*(6), 1045–1068.

Harvard Civil Rights Project. (2005). *Confronting the graduation rate crisis in California.* retrieved November 2, 2010, from http://civilrightsproject.ucla.edu/research/k-12-education/school-dropouts/confronting-the-graduation-rate-crisis-in-california/crp-confronting-dropouts-ca-2005.pdf

Lotan, R. (2008). Developing language and mastering content in heterogeneous classrooms. In R. Gillies, A. Ashman, & J. Terwel (Eds.), *The teacher's role in implementing cooperative learning in the classroom* (pp. 184–200). New York: Springer.

Lucas, S. R. (1999). *Tracking inequality.* New York: Teachers College Press.

Mickelson, R. A. (1999). *The effects of tracking, within-school segregation, and racially identifiable African American schools on student outcomes in the Charlotte-Mecklenburg School District: A report to the U.S. District Court for the Western District of North Carolina in the case of Capacchione v. Charlotte-Mecklenburg Schools et al.* Charlotte, North Carolina.

Woodworth, K. R., David, J. L., Guha, R., Wang, H., & Lopez-Torkos, A. (2008). *San Francisco Bay Area KIPP schools: A study of early implementation and achievement.* Menlo Park: SRI.

Yonezawa, S., Wells, A. S., & Serna, I. (2002). Choosing tracks: "Freedom of choice" in detracking schools. *American Educational Research Journal, 30*(1), 37–67.

Epilogue

Maika Watanabe

This section provides a snapshot of each featured school in 2010, just a few years after we shot footage for the film.

High Tech High Bayshore

The decision to close High Tech High Bayshore came abruptly in February of 2007, without advanced notice to teachers, students, or parents. According to the seven High Tech High teachers with whom I conferred, several interrelated factors contributed to the school's closure. One major cause was the school's enrollment, which was too low to cover its operating costs. In addition, teachers felt that on-site leadership, especially in dealing with struggling students, and institutional support from the High Tech High network in San Diego both could have been stronger. In 2007, High Tech High leaders in San Diego were new to expanding the model beyond their local sites. When faced with a struggling school, leaders and donors may have rethought their decision to invest in a school in Northern California, when their dollars could stretch further nearer to San Diego. High Tech High may have also wanted to "protect the brand" when HTH Bayshore began to implement strategies that were antithetical to the mission of the High Tech High network, most notably by placing students who disrupted classes into a temporary class that did not do project-based learning.

There were additional challenges for High Tech High Bayshore that had to do with its enrollment history. HTH Bayshore absorbed juniors and seniors from another charter school. A few teachers I interviewed reported that some of these students resented the perceived "takeover" by High Tech High Bayshore and did not buy into the High Tech High model, with its emphasis on project-based learning. The neighboring public school district also sent some of their most challenging students to High Tech Bayshore, in response to High Tech High Bayshore's recruitment efforts, whether it was because district administrators believed that the school could be beneficial to these students, or, as some teachers heard, because the school district was not particularly supportive of the charter school. The resulting student population was thus a mix of students who were resentful of the "takeover" and students who were struggling academically, as well as students who were excited by the High Tech High model of instruction. As is true at other public schools, one teacher described how some teachers were more successful at reaching this diverse population, while others struggled with classroom management. Midway through the school year, student attrition became a problem, especially with students who could excel in larger public high schools. Some parents expressed specific concerns about their children being in classrooms with unmotivated students, and/or with children from low socioeconomic backgrounds.

Based on this story, some readers may wonder whether you can successfully teach heterogeneous students in one classroom using the High Tech High approach. High Tech High Bayshore closed, but the High Tech Highs in San Diego are thriving, with a total of nine campuses: These schools typically have four times as many applicants as spots available, and 100% of the graduating class of 2008 was accepted into colleges. These results were achieved with a heterogeneous student population—High Tech High admits students by lottery and strives to get a balance of students from a wide range of socioeconomic strata. A teacher described how the computer-based lottery program selects students by zip code to "make it a non-homogeneous, diverse, heterogeneous population because they're taking kids from each of the zip codes, so you should have students from all sorts of socioeconomic statuses." Two teachers at three San Diego–based High Tech Highs attested to there being all types of students at these schools—some who came in motivated and eager to learn, and others who were not yet accepting of the High Tech High model of instruction. Thus, even with the combination of factors described at High Tech High Bayshore, a longer-term investment into implementing the model, coupled with stronger leadership and organizational support might have allowed school staff to address the challenges it faced.

San Lorenzo High School

Teaching and learning in San Lorenzo High School's math department has changed dramatically since I filmed in 2008. District leadership changed, with a new superintendent in 2007 and a new Director of Secondary Education in 2008. Three teacher leaders, who together had forty years of teaching experience between them, and who had served as department chairs, resigned in 2010, citing frustration with district mandates to change their teaching in ways they believed would harm students' math learning. Teachers were fed up with the lack of teacher input in district-level decision making, as well as the lack of clear, consistent communication on instructional and pedagogical rationales for district mandates. One other young faculty member also decided to leave once his colleagues resigned. Laura Evans, featured prominently in the film, also left at the end of the school year in 2008.

Federal No Child Left Behind (NCLB) legislation makes Title I funding for disadvantaged students contingent on the district's progress in increasing the percentages of students who are proficient in English and mathematics. When schools do not make Adequate Yearly Progress (AYP) for two consecutive years, the district enters into Program Improvement. In 2007, when San Lorenzo Unified School district hired a new superintendent, the district was in year three of Program Improvement, narrowly missing one of the 42 Adequate Yearly Progress indicators during the 2006–2007 school year (San Lorenzo Unified School District, 2010). Exiting Program Improvement by increasing test scores was thus a priority, since if a school does not make Adequate Yearly Progress in four years, NCLB recommends significant restructuring, or even takeover in the fifth year. To respond to the district's concern about the test scores, math faculty carefully documented how the department was including preparation for the high school exit exam and the California Standards Test (CST) for algebra in the curricula.

There were three key flash points in this high-stakes accountability climate that led the teacher leaders to leave. First, the superintendent directed principals to institute 50-minute class periods in place of the blocked schedule, beginning in the fall of 2009 (San Lorenzo Unified School District, 2009), despite vocal opposition from faculty members, who repeatedly asked for research-based rationales for this policy change (see December 16, 2008, school board meeting minutes). As discussed in Chapter 6 above, the blocked schedule was a key factor in why students, even those who began with Algebra in the ninth grade, could reach Calculus as seniors. Without the block schedule, many students would be excluded from advanced college-bound mathematics courses since they could not progress through the sequence of courses to reach Calculus in their four years. Despite their objections to this change, the teachers adapted their curricula to fit the 50-minute class periods, as directed by the district.

Secondly, the district mandated that the department track students into high school math classes based on prior mathematics learning and achievement in middle school. One teacher I interviewed noted, "the beginning of the end for me was the reimposition of tracking." All students who were enrolling in Algebra as ninth graders would simultaneously and automatically enroll in a remedial class titled Algebra "Success." The department instituted this change, as directed by district administrators, but the results were "miserable," according to one teacher. Students did not understand why they were in the Algebra "Success" class while their friends were not. "Kids who were pissed off at being in Algebra 'Success,' that made them pissed off at math and it had been a long, long time since San Lorenzo kids were unhappy as math students, generally," the teacher explained. In contrast, the second semester Algebra B support class under the blocked schedule worked better for two reasons. First, students had a fresh start in high school with a new way of learning mathematics during the first semester. Second, if teachers thought a student would benefit from the Algebra B support class, they had one-on-one meetings with the student about his/her choices—take Algebra A again, or take Algebra B with the support class. The conversations were grounded in specific strengths and weaknesses observed during the first semester, and students were given the chance to opt into the Algebra B support class. "There's no way to have that kind of conversation generically with kids when they start the [Algebra 'Success'] course," a teacher explained.

The final straw for teachers who decided to leave was a communication from the Director of Secondary Education that district administrators rejected the math department's proposal to address the district's test performance goals, and that they "expected to see explicit direct instruction as the primary mode of instruction." One teacher noted that the director "backed down from that but it just sent me over the edge . . . to put in all that time and energy to figure out how to meet the compliance needs of the district and do right for kids and have it summarily rejected without a conversation just felt ridiculous." One of the teacher leaders thought he could no longer, with integrity, recruit new, untenured teachers who could not be shielded from the district mandates. He explained, "I couldn't protect the new people individually and I couldn't protect the work of the department collectively in that kind of setting. I couldn't make it work if there were going to be more extreme fights over direct instruction, . . . over tracking."

I was quite devastated to learn of the collapse of the math department at San Lorenzo High School, as it was when I filmed. The teacher leaders who resigned are extremely dedicated to their students and to math equity, and it was a difficult emotional and financial decision to leave a tenured teaching position with 10 to 20 years of experience and strong roots in the community. One of the teacher leaders I met with on a weekend was still off to a San Lorenzo High School football game after our interview, even though he taught in a different school district after he resigned—the connections with students and the community were that strong.

Summit Prep Charter High School

On a very hopeful note, Summit Prep is receiving national accolades for its student performance. In 2010, *US News and World Report* ranked

Summit Prep #76 in its survey of the country's top public high schools, which places the school

> in the top 0.25 percent of the nation's public high schools. Using the "equity and excellence" rankings that consider how many students take and pass AP exams, Summit ranks 73rd among the nation's nearly 23,000 public schools. This placed Summit 9th in California. . . . (Summit Prep, 2010a)

The Summit statistics were outstanding: 100% of its graduates met the University of California A-G requirements, compared to 40% of students statewide; 75% of seniors passed at least one AP exam, compared to 21% of students in California; and 96% of graduates were accepted to at least one four-year college (Summit, 2010b). The school was also featured in the film *Waiting for Superman,* released in 2010, as an example of a school that did not track students and made phenomenal achievements in preparing students for college. The school has had such a high demand (four times as many applications for spots available in 2010) that the model is expanding. Everest Public High School opened in 2009, modeled after Summit Prep Charter High School.

In 2009, Summit Prep and Everest received a $450,000 grant to provide additional resources around math over four years. School administrators used these funds, in part, to hire two onsite math curricular specialists who help coordinate professional development for math teachers; teach math support, intersession, and summer school classes; conduct in-class observations; conference with math teachers; and survey students about attitudes towards math. The math department chose the following dilemma to focus on in 2010: "How do we support all students to be powerful math learners in our heterogeneous classrooms?" They defined a "powerful math learner" as someone who takes risks, communicates productively, and works persistently.

References

San Lorenzo Unified School District. (2009, June 2). Meeting minutes. Retrieved December 1, 2010, from http://www.slzusd.org/cms/page_view?d=x&piid=&vpid=1240916792459

San Lorenzo Unified School District. (2010). *Program Improvement Information.* Retireved November 15, 2010, from http://www.slzusd.org/cms/page_view?vpid=1241915501820

Summit Prep. (2010a). *Summit in the News.* Retrieved October 25, 2010, from http://www.summitprep.net

Summit Prep. (2010b). *2010–2011 At-a-Glance.* Summit Prep Charter High School.

Recommended Resources on Detracking and Complex Instruction

Maika Watanabe

Burris, C. C., & Garrity, D. T. (2008). ***Detracking for excellence and equity.*** **Alexandria, VA: Association for Supervision and Curriculum Development.**

In the introduction to this book, I mention the compelling research evidence for detracking based on data from the Rockville Centre School District in New York. School principal Carol Burris and Assistant Superintendent Delia Garrity wrote this book chronicling their experience detracking the school district in all subjects through the tenth grade. They provide sage, research-based advice on how to begin the detracking process, how to respond to fear and anxiety from parents and teachers, and how to support teachers through professional development. The district's story is inspiring.

Cohen, E. G. (1994). ***Designing groupwork: Strategies for the heterogeneous classroom*** **(2nd ed.). New York: Teachers College Press.**

This book introduces complex instruction, and the author writes in very practitioner-friendly language, even when discussing research. This book is a must-read for anyone interested in implementing complex instruction, as you hear Elizabeth Cohen's voice as she defines groupwork, provides the rationale for groupwork, and describes the dilemmas of groupwork, including status hierarchies. Chapters on implementing complex instruction include how to develop group norms, how to create tasks, how to develop and assign roles, how to assign competence, and how to evaluate groupwork. One of the best resources for teachers is the appendix of "Cooperative Training Exercises," which provides puzzles for students to figure out in teams. These exercises are excellent conversation starters on group norms.

Cohen, E. G., & Lotan, R. A. (Eds.). (1997). *Working for equity in heterogeneous classrooms: Sociological theory in practice.* New York: Teachers College Press.

This book presents the sociological theory behind complex instruction as well as 20 years of research on complex instruction as practiced in varied school settings. This book is for anyone who wants research evidence for the effectiveness of complex instruction in classrooms. Amidst all of the statistical tables and figures, the chapters also feature in-depth descriptions of the teachers' complex instruction units and fieldnote entries that make the students' and teachers' responses come alive.

Fine, M., Anand, B. T., Jordan, C. P., & Sherman, D. (1998). *Off track: Classroom privilege for all.* New York: Teachers College Press.

This 30-minute film inspired the making of *"Heterogenius" Classrooms. "Off Track"* features a detracked high school English classroom. The voices of students are especially powerful as they reflect on their positive experiences with detracking reform.

Oakes, J. (2005). *Keeping track: How schools structure inequality* (2nd ed.). New Haven, CT: Yale University Press.

Jeannie Oakes, the most widely cited scholar on tracking, first published this book in 1985. This book is a "must-read" for anyone pursuing detracking reform, as it provided the foundation and the impetus for detracking reform. Chapter 1 very eloquently debunks commonly held assumptions regarding tracking. Chapter 2 places tracking in a historical context. Chapters 3–8 describe qualitative and quantitative research undertaken by Oakes and her colleagues that examines tracking at 25 schools across the country. She analyzes the differing opportunities to learn and classroom climates across tracks, describing them in the teachers' and students' own words. There is also a chapter on the constitutionality of tracking. The 2005 edition includes astute chapters on two decades of research on tracking and detracking since she first published *Keeping Track.* The "Tracking Wars" chapter addresses the debate over detracking, and the final chapter provides compelling case studies of schools that have taken on the challenge of detracking to provide equitable instructional opportunities for all students.

Rubin, B. C. (Ed.). (2006). Detracking and heterogeneous grouping [Special issue]. *Theory into Practice,* 45(1).

This special issue of *Theory into Practice* presents the latest research on detracking in short, easily readable articles. The first, "Engaging Beliefs," features articles on student and teacher perspectives on detracking. The second section, "Engaging Practice," describes detracking in math, science, English, and social studies classrooms. The third section, "Engaging Structure and Politics," provides lessons learned from departments and schools that have detracked.

Shulman, J., Lotan, R., & Whitcomb, J. (Eds.). (1998). ***Groupwork in diverse classrooms: A casebook for educators.*** **New York: Teachers College Press.**

I highly recommend this book, as well as its companion facilitator's guide, for any teacher inquiry group and for teacher educators, as it provides case-based starting points for discussion on groupwork. The book features the voices of sixteen practitioners, relating their dilemmas, challenges, and successes as they implemented groupwork. Each case provides a first-hand account of handling a particular issue, such as the dilemma about when to intervene, or whether the teacher should let kids fail or not.

Watanabe, M. (2007). Lessons from a teacher inquiry group about tracking: Perceived student choice in course-taking and its implications for detracking reform. ***Teachers College Record, 109*****(9), 2136–2170.**

This article reports on lessons learned from a year-long teacher inquiry into detracking, ability, and intelligence with six teachers from a college-preparatory urban high school that historically disavowed tracking. The teachers met once or twice a month for a school year. I would recommend this article to any teacher or administrator who wants to begin a conversation about detracking with colleagues, to avoid our mistakes and to dig deeply into challenging conversations. The article recommends topics for teachers to grapple with, including clearly defining tracking in relation to a specific school context. In our teacher inquiry group, we met for seven months before realizing that we had differing conceptions of what tracking was and was not.

Watanabe, M. (2007). Tracking. In S. Mathison & E. W. Ross (Eds.), ***Battleground schools*** **(pp. 671–679). Westport, CT: Greenwood/Praeger.**

This short article summarizes the controversy over tracking and detracking, presenting both sides of the debate. This entry specifically summarizes the research on the effect of detracking on student achievement for students formerly in the low, middle, and high tracks.

Watanabe, M. (Ed.). (2008). Tracking and detracking in the era of accountability [Special issue]. ***Teachers College Record, 110*****(3).**

This special issue of *Teachers College Record* examines the complexities of organizing schools as tracked or detracked environments in the new era of high-stakes testing. Some schools and school districts are maintaining tracking, others are tracking more, and still others are detracking, with varied instructional and student achievement outcomes. Two articles in the issue, one written by Carol Burris, Ed Wiley, Kevin Welner, and John Murphy, and another written by Jo Boaler and Megan Staples, include research evidence that detracking helps all students and can eliminate achievement gaps.

Wheelock, A. (1992). ***Crossing the tracks: How "untracking" can save America's schools.*** **New York: The New Press.**

This book is a very practical guide for those interested in starting a conversation about detracking, with especially well-written chapters on how to get parents, community members, and teachers on board to detrack. The book also includes chapters on instruction and assessment. It is filled with testimony from educators across the country who have detracked, and includes helpful tips such as "Preparing for Tough Questions: What do you say when . . . ?"

Film Credits, Acknowledgments and Contact Information

Project Director/Video Producer:
Maika Watanabe, Associate Professor, Department of Secondary Education, San Francisco State University
Videography by:
Maura Devlin-Clancy
Ben Fendel
Additional Camerawork by:
Maika Watanabe
Sarah Gilson
Editing by:
Conor Gordon
Sarah Gilson
Additional editing by:
Ben Fendel
Maura Devlin-Clancy
Music by:
Conor Gordon
Graphics by:
Sarah Gilson
Additional Graphics by:
Maura Devlin-Clancy
Special thanks to:
Laura Evans, San Lorenzo High School
Rachel Lotan, Stanford University
Maja Catipovic, High Tech High Bayshore
Todd Dickson, Summit Prep High School
Howard Shen, Summit Prep High School
Jon Deane, Summit Prep High School
Feroze Munshi, High Tech High Bayshore
Nicci Nunes, UC Berkeley
Carol Burris, South Side High School
Conor Gordon, San Francisco State University
Additional thanks to:
Students at High Tech High Bayshore
Students at Summit Prep High School
Students at San Lorenzo High School
Carlos Cabana, San Lorenzo High School
Mary B. Scott, San Francisco State University
Jonathan Foerster, San Francisco State University
Barbara Shreve, San Lorenzo High School
Cahill Learning Resources and Media Lab Staff, San Francisco State University
Michelle Fine, The Graduate Center of the City University of New York

For more information, contact
Maika Watanabe, San Francisco State University—watanabe@sfsu.edu

About the Contributors

Maika Watanabe is an Associate Professor in the Department of Secondary Education at San Francisco State University, where she has been teaching pre-service teaching credential students since 2003. In addition to teaching courses, Maika supervises student teachers at middle and high schools in the San Francisco Bay Area. Maika earned her B.A. and teaching credential from Swarthmore College, and her M.A. and Ph.D. from UC Berkeley. Prior to graduate school, Maika taught middle school social studies and high school history in California and North Carolina. She is founder and former chair of the American Educational Research Association Special Interest Group on Tracking and Detracking. When Maika is not working, she enjoys exploring San Francisco with her husband and two children.

Maja Catipovic has taught math and physics at Marin School of Arts and Technology, High Tech High Bayshore, Alameda High School, and Island High School, all in the San Francisco Bay Area. She earned her B.S. and B.A. at Brown University and her teaching credential at San Francisco State University. In her spare time, she and her husband enjoy hiking with their dog, cooking tasty, spicy food, and traveling—back home to Europe to spend time with her family on the beaches of Croatia, to visit coffee-houses in Vienna, where she grew up, or to new places off the beaten path.

Laura Evans taught mathematics at San Lorenzo High School for 10 years, using groupwork and complex instruction to teach heterogeneous groups of students. She enjoys supporting teachers interested in cooperative learning and has led professional development workshops in groupwork for the Teachers Development Group, Thrive Foundation for Youth, and the Center for Innovative Teaching and Learning. Throughout her career, she has been a cooperating teacher and a supervisor of student teachers through the Stanford Teacher Education Program. She has also acted as a curriculum and instruction coach at San Lorenzo High School, East Palo Alto High School, and now Summit High School in Redwood City. Laura received her B.S. in Mathematics from California State University, East Bay, and her M.A. and teaching credential from Stanford University. In her spare time, Laura enjoys spending time with her husband and two children.

Howard Shen began teaching at Summit Prep Charter High School in 2006, after graduating from Stanford University with a B.S. in Chemistry, a minor in Computer Science, and an M.A. in Education. Howard was a student teacher at Summit in 2005–06 and has taught both Biology and Chemistry at Summit. Even as a "veteran" teacher at Summit, Howard indulges in his hobbies from adolescence: reading fantasy novels, playing video games, and baking desserts. Howard ascribes strongly to the philosophy that every student can learn Chemistry.

Angela Knotts received her Master's degree in Mathematics Education from Stanford University. Since then, she has taught all levels of secondary mathematics at Sequoia High School, Stanford College Prep, Summit Preparatory Charter High School, and Buchser Middle School. In addition to teaching math, she has also been involved with many facets of pre-service and in-service teacher training and development, serving as a Cooperating Teacher for teacher candidates from Stanford University as well as collaboratively designing and leading professional development workshops in differentiation, complex instruction, interdisciplinary instruction, assessment, and the use of technology in the math classroom. She works regularly with the Performance Assessment for California Teachers program as a scorer and trainer, and also does freelance curriculum design in mathematics.

Jon Deane is the founding Executive Director of Everest Public High School. Jon graduated from Stanford with a Bachelor's degree in Economics, and had a successful first career in finance and accounting, earning his CPA license. He then made a career switch and went back to Stanford for a Master's degree in Education. Jon was at Summit for four years where he taught math and served as the school's Chief Financial Officer. Prior to working at Summit Prep, Jon taught math at East Palo Alto (CA) High School and Prospect Hill Academy Charter School in Cambridge, MA, where he coached the co-ed soccer team to consecutive undefeated seasons.

Jon's passion is finding new ways to help students reach their highest potential, and he is excited to work with the faculty, students, and parents in the Everest community to continue building a school where all students have incredible educational opportunities. When Jon isn't at school with the Snow Leopards, he is usually spending time with his wife, his daughter, and his dog. Jon enjoys running, golfing, and relaxing with a jigsaw puzzle.